How to grow your eCommerce business

By Trevor Ginn

First published in 2022

Vendlab Publishing
2 Spring Valley Business Centre, Porters Wood
St Albans, AL3 6PD, UK

www.vendlab.com/ecommerce-book

hello@vendlab.com

Paperback ISBN 978-1-7391579-4-4

eBook ISBN 978-1-7391579-5-1

FOREWORD

Building a successful eCommerce business is challenging. Low barriers to entry mean that competition is fierce and entrepreneurs must work hard and innovate to stay ahead of the pack. There is massive competition on the major marketing channels and a race to the bottom in terms of margins.

To succeed, retail entrepreneurs need to use the entire arsenal of tools at their disposal, be that online marketplaces, Search Engine Optimisation, Social Media or email marketing. However, many businesses hold themselves back by sticking to what they know. For example, only 15% of retailers in the UK sell cross-border[1]. These sellers are missing a massive opportunity as over 20% of trade is international on platforms such as eBay.

This book will show you all the techniques and know-how needed to grow your online business to a multi-million turnover.

I will teach you how to turn your niche eCommerce store into a multi-channel business with customers worldwide.

In doing this, I draw on my 15 years of hard-won, hands-on experience of running a successful online retailing business and helping other companies grow as a consultant.

---

1   https://www.british-business-bank.co.uk/wp-content/uploads/2020/02/UK-SME-Exporting-FINAL-VERSION.pdf

This book has eleven chapters, each with a different eCommerce topic area. Chapters 1 and 2 deal with the nitty-gritty of running an eCommerce business. Chapters 3 to 10 look at the online sales channels and techniques you should be using to grow your business. These chapters cover selling via marketplaces like eBay and Amazon, promoting your business on Google and Facebook and encouraging return customers through email and affiliate marketing.

About Me

My name is Trevor Ginn and I am the founder of Hello Baby, an online retailer based in the UK focusing on the preschool space.

I built Hello Baby from scratch to a turnover of £5m/year with no external funding. It has been hard work but rewarding!

I also run Vendlab.com, an eCommerce consultancy specialising in helping eCommerce businesses grow through multi-channel eCommerce.

Along the way, I have picked up a wealth of knowledge about eCommerce and how to build a small business. In this book, I have tried to distil all I have learned on my journey to help you grow your online business.

Stay in Touch

It is hard and sometimes lonely running your own business. With this in mind, I have launched a Facebook group so that readers of this book can connect:

https://www.facebook.com/groups/vendlab

If you require more help on the topics in this book, check out my online courses:

https://vendlab.com/ecommerce-courses/

I also host the *eCommerce Odyssey* podcast on all things eCommerce

https://vendlab.com/podcasts/

And a Youtube Channel:

https://www.youtube.com/c/VendlabeCommerceSchool

Trevor Ginn
St Albans, UK. 2022
trevor@vendlab.com

CONTENTS

PART I:

THE BUSINESS OF eCOMMERCE

Building an eCommerce business requires a breadth of skills. Firstly, you must be an expert at running a physical business, which means managing pricing, stock and selecting products that people want to buy. Secondly, you must also be on top of a constantly growing array of platforms and techniques for driving traffic and converting browsers into customers. The variety of skills required makes eCommerce exciting, but it also makes it hard to get right.

In Chapters 1 and 2, we look at how to win at the business of eCommerce. In Chapter 1, we take a bird's eye view of the strategies eCommerce businesses use to succeed. Then, in Chapter 2, we look at measuring and understanding your business performance.

Chapter 1: Paths to growth

Fundamentally there are only three ways in which companies (including eCommerce businesses) grow:

1. Attract new customers
2. Improve average order value
3. Drive repeat purchases

Chapter 1 looks at strategies for improving performance in each area and discusses how eCommerce businesses use them to grow their business. The platforms and techniques discussed will be covered in more detail in Parts 2 and 3 of this book.

Chapter 2: Improving business performance

The famous scientist Lord Kelvin[2] once said, "If you cannot measure it, you cannot control it." Without monitoring your business' performance, you will not know where you are heading. In Chapter 2,

---

2   https://en.wikipedia.org/wiki/William_Thomson,_1st_Baron_Kelvin

we look at how to measure the performance of your online business. We also look at fundamental metrics like margin and product sell-through rate and ask how these can be improved through smarter ordering and inventory management.

1:

PATHS TO GROWTH

Setting up an eCommerce business has never been easier. Services like Shopify[3] have made launching an eCommerce-enabled business simple and Amazon has created a sales machine so compelling that many sellers do not bother selling anywhere else. In addition, inventory is readily available, with Alibaba[4] providing access to an almost unbelievably extensive range of products. eCommerce is the future of retail and the Covid pandemic merely accelerated an existing trend.

Whilst starting a business is easy, growing them is hard, no matter what market you are in. Online retail is already highly competitive and getting more complicated all the time as new and established businesses enter the market.

In this chapter, we look at strategies for growing an eCommerce business. These can be divided into platforms (e.g. Amazon, eBay, eCommerce website) and techniques (e.g. Search Engine Optimisation, email marketing) that can be used to acquire new customers and retain existing ones.

---

3   https://www.shopify.com
4   https://www.alibaba.com

Fundamentals of growing a business

Whether you are a mom-and-pop store or an international brand, all businesses have the same three options available to grow their business. These are[5]:

1. Attract new prospects and convert them to customers.
2. Increase the average transaction value.
3. Encourage existing customers to order more frequently.

eCommerce businesses are no exception. They live and die on their success at driving traffic from new or existing customers and then converting it into sales. The process is summarised in this simple equation:

Traffic × Average Order Value × Conversion Rate = Gross Merchandising Volume
(AOV) **(GMV)**

In this chapter, we look at each of these sections in turn:

1. Attracting new customers

There are two sources of traffic that eCommerce businesses can harness:

- **Driving traffic to your website from paid or organic (e.g. free) sources.** Sources of traffic include Paid Search and Search Engine Optimisation.
- **3rd party platforms.** By selling through marketplaces, such as eBay and Amazon, you can reach hundreds of millions of customers all over the world.

---

[5]   https://www.abraham.com/topic/three-ways-to-grow-your-business

Once you have attracted potential customers, you need to convert them into buyers. Improving your conversion rate, either on your website or on third-party listings, will reduce your cost of advertising and increase your sales. This can be achieved by measuring your performance through web analytics packages, e.g. Google Analytics, and applying usability best practices.

2. Improving Average Order Value

Improving your average order value will increase revenue from the same number of customers, boosting profitability if costs stay constant. Average order value can be enhanced through promotions, such as free shipping over a minimum purchase threshold or changing your mix of products to increase your average ticket price.

3. Retention marketing

When eCommerce businesses start, they typically focus on acquiring new customers. Doing this is easy if you do not mind paying for advertising on Google or Facebook. However, whilst it is always important to acquire customers, it is up to five times more expensive to sell to a new customer than an existing one[6].

Attracting new customers by driving traffic

Driving new customers to your products or services is critical to eCommerce businesses. There are multiple ways to reach potential customers online. These include:

- **Selling multi-platform.** You can reach customers where they prefer to shop by selling through multiple online platforms. For example, research shows that consumers' first choice

---

6   https://www.invespcro.com/blog/customer-acquisit on-retention

for product search is Amazon (41%), followed by Google (28%)[7].

- **Driving website traffic – paid promotion.** Buying adverts on major online marketing platforms, e.g. Google search and Facebook, to drive traffic to your website and products.
- **Driving website traffic – 'organic' promotion.** Posting content online to drive unpaid 'organic' traffic to your site. This could be content on your website to drive traffic via Google natural search or content on Social Media networks like Facebook.
- **Expand internationally.** It is a big world out there! By promoting your products internationally, you can double your sales.

When driving traffic, it is essential to ensure that the maximum number of browsers are converted into buyers. This is true on your website and your third-party marketplace listings. In addition, you should constantly monitor and improve your online performance. This can be achieved by measuring your performance using web analytics packages like Google Analytics and implementing usability best practices (see Chapter 3).

Selling multi-platform

When making a purchase online, consumers can choose to visit an individual retailer's website (frequently via a Google search) or purchase from one of a few high-traffic marketplaces. Of course, both websites and marketplaces have their advantages.

My retail business is massively multi-platform and we have found that adding new platforms is one of the easiest and most cost-effective ways to increase sales. For example, if you are already selling on Amazon

---

7   https://www.mediagrouponlineinc.com/wp-content/uploads/2018/09/
     Sept18NewMedia_Amazon-Now-Tops-Google-for-Product-Searches_
     FINAL.pdf

UK or in the US, offering the same inventory on Amazon Canada will introduce your products to new customers. While new platforms can cannibalise existing channels, these customers would often be hard to reach. For example, it is challenging for a UK business to get customers in Japan other than via Amazon Japan.

Often, a consumer's only preference boils down to convenience and price. Therefore, if you are not selling your products across platforms, you could lose sales to a more diversified competitor. Furthermore, consumers are increasingly using a range of different platforms and devices to make purchases. Here are some multi-platform eCommerce facts:

- **Marketplaces.** Amazon now accounts for 50% of the US eCommerce market, up from 38% in 2015 (Source: eMarketer)[8]. eBay is also a significant market force.
- **Mobile-first.** 60% of all eCommerce traffic now occurs on a mobile device. (Source: Salesforce/Publicis)[9]
- **Get social.** 60% of Instagram users say they discover new products on Instagram. (Source: Instagram)[10]

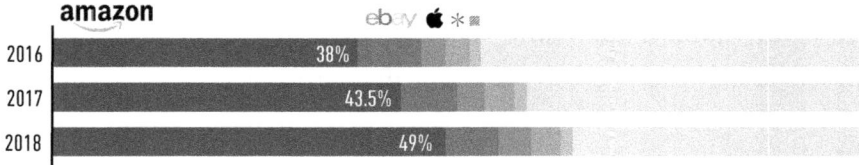

Fig. 1. Multi-channel sales (Source: Visual Capitalist)[11]

---

8   https://www.emarketer.com/content/amazon-now-has-nearly-50-of-us-ecommerce-market

9   https://www.retailtimes.co.uk/wp-content/uploads/2018/08/Shopper-First-Retailing-2-1-1.pdf

10   https://business.instagram.com/getting-started/#why-instagram

11   https://www.visualcapitalist.com/chart-shows-amazons-dominance-ecommerce

As shown in the diagram above, eCommerce platforms such as Amazon and eBay are rising in popularity and control over half the eCommerce marketplace. The takeaway message here is that you exclude your business from half of the market when you avoid marketplaces or only sell on marketplaces.

Increasing the number of platforms through which you sell exposes your products to more customers, promotes your brand and increases sales. Conversely, a single-platform approach cuts off your business from a wealth of potential customers. I strongly recommend a multi-channel approach as this maximises sales and minimises risk. If you depend too much on one traffic source, you put too many eggs in one basket. For example, Amazon can and does shut seller accounts for little reason and this can be disastrous for the many businesses which rely solely on this platform.

Marketplaces

Marketplace platforms like Amazon have a vast, international user base. They are great for driving sales volume, both domestically and internationally. They are also easy to set up and use. On the flip side, when selling on the marketplace, you do not 'own' the customer and cannot market to them directly. They also charge high fees. For these reasons, many retailers avoid online marketplaces.

Online marketplaces, such as eBay and Amazon, provide an all-in-one solution for merchants to reach customers. Marketplaces are an excellent way for sellers to get their foot in the door online and are also a fast way to build sales and generate initial brand awareness. As a result, many sellers start on marketplaces before selling through a website or even an offline store. Marketplaces offer the following benefits to sellers:

- **Huge audience.** Marketplaces have millions of daily users.
- **Secure payments.** Online payments are managed by the marketplace, reducing the risk of fraud.

- **Advertising.** On top of natural search performance on the marketplace, merchants can buy additional advertising to boost their exposure and sales.

On the negative side, the marketplace will 'own' the customer and typically does not allow the merchant to market to the customer directly. We will cover marketplaces in more detail in Chapters 9, 10 and 11.

Websites

The ease of selling through sites like eBay and Amazon means that some sellers only sell through marketplaces. However, with the advent of fully-managed website services, such as Shopify[12] and Wix[13], it has never been easier to set up and run a website of your very own. These platforms are websites and eCommerce platforms for which a whole ecosystem of third-party apps is available. Selling through a website has the following advantages:

- **More control.** Nobody can shut down your website! Also, unlike marketplaces, you 'own' any customers sold to via your website, enabling you to market to them in the future.
- **Reach more customers.** Many online marketing techniques, e.g. Google and Facebook Ads, require a transactional website to complete the sale. Adverts on these platforms drive traffic to your website, where the sale will occur.

Marketing techniques for growing website sales are explained in Chapters 4 to 7.

---

12   https://www.shopify.com

13   https://www.wix.com

Expanding internationally

I am a big fan of international trade and my business exports around 50% of its sales. However, while this is perhaps on the high side (I'd like us to increase sales domestically), most retailing businesses could increase sales by 10-20% by selling internationally!

One of the easiest ways to expand internationally is through marketplaces. Some marketplaces are international in scope (e.g. eBay and Amazon), whilst others have a strong regional focus (e.g. Bol.com[14] in the Netherlands and Cdiscount[15] in France). However, sending orders overseas is more complex and riskier than domestically. Marketplaces make life easier for sellers as they handle order processing, payment and (if required) fulfilment. By giving delivery and payment guarantees, they also mitigate risk and provide peace of mind for buyers and sellers.

Another great way of gaining international exposure is via Google Shopping. Google's shopping programme can promote products to customers in nearly 100 countries[16]. For customer service, use Google Translate. It works surprisingly well!

Building a brand

Competition is fierce online and many markets are saturated. To have any hope of standing out, you will need to develop a recognisable and memorable brand. Branding is a significant factor for consumers when they make a purchase decision. About 60% of shoppers actively buy from brands they know and 21% purchase products because they like the brand (Source: Nielsen[17]).

---

14   https://www.bol.com
15   https://www.cdiscount.com
16   https://support.google.com/merchants/answer/160637
17   https://www.invespcro.com/blog/how-branding-influences-purchase-decisions-infographic

While a brand is classically a name and a visual identity (i.e. a logo), it also broadly refers to a customer's experience when dealing with a brand as a shopper, customer or Social Media follower.

Developing your brand

Good branding will lead to awareness, recognition, trust and revenue. If your brand does not connect with your audience, it will not achieve these goals. Before developing your brand, ask the following questions:

- Who is your target audience?
- What is your product niche?
- What makes you unique?

There are probably lots of competitors in your industry and niche. Think about what makes you different. What values, benefits and qualities make your brand unique? How do your products improve lives and contribute to success?

Choosing a name and URL

When launching a business or a new brand, you will need to select a URL for your website and usernames for marketplaces and Social Media accounts.

When choosing, select a different name from other competitors in your space as this will increase your online findability. With the proliferation of online businesses, this is becoming more difficult but keep trying until you succeed. Here are some general pointers for selecting a name and a URL for your business:

- **Keep it short.** Long and complicated names are easy to forget. Always choose something which rolls off the tongue.
- **Easy to interpret.** Ideally, someone can look at your name or URL and quickly guess what your company does.

- **Target broad keywords.** Including keywords in your domain can help your natural search engine performance.
- **Make the URL and name easy to say and remember.** Avoid any difficult and foreign words. Avoid numbers and punctuation, e.g. dashes.

In terms of your domain name, .com is preferable for commercial sites as it is seen as broadly territory neutral. This will help if you are offering your products overseas.

Create a visual identity

It is advisable to employ a professional graphic designer to develop a professional-looking logo and visual identity. A set of brand guidelines (or a brand style guide) will ensure that your branding is applied accurately and consistently.

Put your branding to work

Aim for consistent implementation of your brand across your business, including all customer touchpoints, such as:

- Your website
- Marketplace accounts
- Social media accounts
- Marketing communications, e.g. email, flyers
- Customer service communication, e.g. support emails
- Packaging and packing inserts

Strong brand identity also acts as a unifying factor across all your online channels. Depending on their customer journey, the same customer might buy from your company through Amazon, eBay or your website. Here is how my company uses the same identity across multiple platforms:

- **Website:** www.hellobabydirect.com
- **eBay:** www.ebay.co.uk/str/hellobabydirect
- **Facebook:** www.facebook.com/hellobabydirect
- **Twitter:** www.twitter.com/hellobabydirect
- **Pinterest:** www.pinterest.co.uk/hellobabyonline
- **Amazon:** Hello Baby

Driving website traffic – 'organic' promotion

The major online publishing platforms, i.e. Google and the Social Media platforms, promote users' content for free. This could be in posts on Facebook and Instagram or Google's search engine serving up a link to a website to answer a user's query. As traffic is a precious resource, businesses should maximise free traffic. However, generating traffic is hard work and requires, amongst other things, regular posting of high-quality content.

Search Engine Optimisation

This is the process of configuring your website to appear well-placed in the unpaid (a.k.a. natural or organic) search results for relevant queries. For example, if you are a seller of speciality tea, you might want your website to come up on top when someone searches for 'herbal tea' or 'loose-leaf tea'. However, although this traffic is notionally 'free', building performance is challenging. As a result, many companies will outsource this to specialist external agencies.

With 92% of the search market, Google is the biggest search engine in the West and the average user makes between 3 and 4 Google searches a day (Source: HubSpot).[18] Consequently, every business should be using Google to connect with these potential customers. Businesses can reach new customers on Google by configuring their site to perform well in the 'organic' (i.e. free) search results. They can also pay for exposure by buying adverts next to the organic search results (see paid search below).

---

18   https://blog.hubspot.com/marketing/google-search-statistics

There are several opportunities to obtain free traffic from Google, focusing on different media types. These include:

- **Search.** This is what people generally mean when they talk about Google search. The general search results focus on the site's textual content.
- **Shopping.** Google's shopping search has both a free and a paid element. By submitting a product feed, (i.e. a file containing product data, prices and stock level), you can access a certain amount of free traffic, although paid ads get the best position and attract the lion's share of clicks.
- **Local search.** Many searches are local in nature and, by creating a Google Places profile, you can get your businesses featured for local searches.
- **Image search.** Google has a dedicated image search tab. By labelling your images correctly, you can obtain a large proportion of your traffic from this source.

Social Media

Social Media platforms, like Facebook, have billions of users worldwide and are unbeatable for connecting with your audience. They allow businesses to communicate with users and drive traffic through unpaid or 'organic' posts and paid ads.

Businesses can create a profile, post content and build up a following for free on Social Media platforms like Facebook. Facebook and Instagram also provide a 'shop' for merchants, but no checkout is available, so purchases are completed by visiting the merchant's website. However, it is only a matter of time before these platforms will give customers the option to check out without leaving their platform.

Social Media marketing is covered in more detail in Chapter 8.

Driving website traffic – paid promotion

To get customers to your website, you will probably end up buying a large proportion of your traffic one way or another. There are multiple opportunities online for paying to promote your products. Savvy businesses will use most, if not all, of them to get in front of customers when researching products to buy.

Paid Search

Building organic traffic is a long and uncertain process. Therefore, Google offers to display ads alongside organic results to businesses looking for quicker results. These ads are charged on a pay-per-click (PPC) basis and are easy to set up and manage. While PPC costs can be high, Google Ads are the primary way to reach customers for many businesses. In addition, Google Ads targets customers as they research products to buy, so they can be highly efficient.

Alongside Google, Microsoft's search engine, Bing, offers a similar search ads programme. Bing has only a tiny proportion of the market, but the ads can be cheaper and there is less competition.

Paid search is covered in detail in Chapter 5.

Social media advertising

The sheer volume of content on Social Media platforms makes it difficult for organic posts to be seen by anything more than a small proportion of your target audience. Consequently, all the major Social Media platforms run advertising programmes to enable businesses to buy exposure. Adverts can be used for several purposes:

- **'Boost' content.** Drive traffic to posts within the platform to increase readership and attract followers.
- **Advertise products.** Drive traffic to external sites where products can be purchased.

The information that Social Media platforms hold about their users enables advertisers to laser-target adverts in a way that has just not been possible in the past. When creating campaigns, advertisers can segment users by location, interests and demographics to reach their target customer.

Affiliate marketing

Affiliate marketing is where a website (the publisher) directs traffic to a merchant's website (the advertiser) and gains a commission if a purchase is made. For example, Amazon runs a programme called 'Amazon Associates' where websites linking to Amazon via a unique link can get a commission if a sale is made.

Affiliate marketing is a great way to increase your exposure across the internet. As payments are usually commission-based, they are low risk and easy to set up.

Affiliate marketing is covered in Chapter 6.

Improving conversion rate

It is not enough to drive traffic to your products; you must also turn those browsers into customers. Conversion rate refers to the proportion of browsers that make a purchase. At each stage of by buying process, the browser will decide whether to progress to the next step. Examples include:

- **Clicking on an entry from a list of search results.** This could be on Google or a marketplace like eBay or Amazon.
- **Clicking 'Buy' on a product page.** Again, this could be on a website or a marketplace.
- **Checkout completion.** Progressing through each stage of a checkout process.

There will be a percentage of dropouts at each step in the process. You will increase your eventual number of buyers by improving performance at each journey stage. Improving the conversion rate of the traffic you receive will reduce your cost of sales and improve profitability. Driving traffic is hard work and expensive, so make the most out of it!

Conversion rate is a significant success factor on websites and on marketplaces where the quality of the product listings determines the click-through and conversion rates. Many factors influence the conversion rate:

- **Usability.** How easy is it for your customer to make a purchase? Are there any points along the journey where they often drop out?
- **Trust.** How trustworthy is your brand? Does your store have good reviews?
- **Price.** Consumers are very price-sensitive, so you need to be competitive to stay in the game.
- **Offer.** Price is important, but customers also consider other factors such as speed of delivery and ease of returns.
- **Product data.** Products cannot be handled online, so improving the quality of your product images and descriptions will help turn browsers into buyers.
- **Customer service.** Companies, e.g. Zappos, have made customer service a unique selling point, going to absurd lengths to keep people happy. Whilst you do not need to go that far, excellent customer service is a wonderful way of improving conversion rate and increasing the number of returning customers. Simple changes like adding a phone number can make a big difference.

Website Usability

Website usability is all about making the customer's purchasing journey as easy as possible. There are lots of factors to consider, including:

- **Navigation.** How easy is it to find products on your site?
- **Search.** Does your search function generate good results?
- **Mobile.** Most users now make purchases through mobile devices. Is your site mobile-friendly?
- **Website performance.** How quickly does your website load?
- **Checkout.** Is your checkout process quick and easy?

We cover website usability and tracking website performance in Chapter 3.

Availability

Being available to answer queries is a great way to boost trust. By adding a phone number and website chat, you can reassure customers that you are an established business that will solve customer queries quickly. Of course, you should always provide a contact email.

Branding

Having a recognisable, distinctive brand will build trust in your business. While many online companies, especially marketplace sellers, will trade under a generic name (e.g. XYZ trading), it is best to invest in developing a distinctive brand that identifies your business and helps build customer loyalty and increase repeat business.

Offer

Price is a significant factor in online purchasing decisions, but it is far from the only one. The market is saturated with goods and services and it is a challenge to offer something unique. Consider carefully what makes your offer special. List how customers will benefit from your products and define the advantages that distinguish you from competitors.

Elements of your offer include:

- **Price** (see below).
- **Delivery time.** Customers love quick, reliable delivery.
- **Return period.** Going above and beyond the statutory return period will reassure customers.
- **Packaging.** Quality packaging and helpful inserts will make your delivery more memorable.

Product data

I am constantly surprised at the dubious quality of product data published online. Many products have short descriptions and poor-quality photos. Giving your product pages high-quality, comprehensive descriptions will provide customers with the information they need, increase your conversion rate and reduce customer service queries. Google loves original content, so longer form content will also improve your natural search engine performance.

Ideally, you would create unique content for all your products. However, this is hugely time-consuming and expensive. So, if this is not possible, focus on your top-selling products and ensure they have top-notch descriptions that give the customer all the information they need.

Pricing

Like it or hate it, pricing is crucial in purchasing decisions. If you are not selling unique products, the chances are that you will be competing with multiple companies for each sale. Even if you sell your own brand, competing products will be available and the price will still be an essential factor. Some facts about online pricing:

- 80% of customers said that price is the most critical factor in purchasing.
- 90% of shoppers hunt for a better deal using online search, marketplaces and comparison-shopping engines.

- Price comparison engines account for 20% of eCommerce traffic. [19]

Customers use search engines when looking for the best deals online. This might be Google's general search, Google shopping search, Amazon or eBay. These search engines all use price as a ranking factor for offers. As a result, the top offer gets the lion's share of sales and will often be only slightly cheaper than the second-placed offer. For example, on Amazon, the Featured or 'Buy-Box' offer can be just £0.01 cheaper than the second-placed item but will capture 83% of the sales[20].

By monitoring your competitors' prices and then adjusting prices both up and down, your business can gain a competitive advantage in the market. This is known as dynamic pricing. However, getting the right balance is tricky. Too high and you will get no sales; too low and you will make no money.

Dynamic pricing (a.k.a. repricing) is a successful eCommerce pricing strategy in which sellers set flexible prices by considering costs, targeted profit margins, market demand and competitors' prices. Repricing is possible on several platforms, including Amazon, Google Shopping and eBay. For each platform, a seller will set a floor price at their minimum acceptable margin and aim to be the best price down to that level.

Manually adjusting prices is very time-consuming. Fortunately, several online dynamic repricing systems[21] track competitor prices and adjust prices according to preset rules. Using different pricing strategies

---

19   https://prisync.com/blog/ultimate-ecommerce-pricing-strategies

20   https://www.repricerexpress.com/win-amazon-buy-box

21   For example, www.boostmyshop.com, www.sniffie.io. These systems tend are charged on a monthly or yearly licence

makes it possible to adjust pricing to maximise your profit or sales. Example rules:

- Be the cheapest in the market.
- Price 5% lower than the market average.
- Price £0.01 below the cheapest.

For example, a retailer on Amazon sells Sophie the Giraffe, a popular baby toy. They have set their floor price at £9.99, which they have calculated to be a 5% margin after all costs (cost prices, VAT, shipping, Amazon fees) are considered. They have set a rule where they will undercut the price of the lowest Prime seller by £0.01 down to £9.99 but ignore other sellers as their offer is Prime eligible. Prime is Amazon's program where members get free next-day delivery on all orders. Prime members often filter for Prime eligible items over non-Prime offers.

The cheapest Prime offer for this item is £10.81, so the retailer prices their offer at £10.80. This wins them the Buy-Box (see Chapter 9 on Amazon), which means they will get the lion's share of the sale for this product.

Experimentation will be required to find the strategy which maximises profit. It could be that being the cheapest by a small margin will generate the most sales. Alternatively, it could be that your brand is strong enough that you merely need to match the lowest price. Matching prices can be preferable, preventing a race to the bottom as merchants undercut each other.

Trust

Building trust around your business is an essential part of conversion rate optimisation. You should demonstrate that you are a reputable business on all your sales channels and throughout all your customer interactions. Areas to reinforce trust include:

Provide Information

Demonstrate to customers that you are an established business by giving them detailed information about your business. This can be as simple as ensuring you have an About Us section on how the company started and what it stands for. You could also have a company blog that shares company news.

Design and branding

Take care to present a unified design and brand across your sale channels and customer touchpoints. As well as your online presence, this includes emails, packaging and flyers.

Reviews and feedback

As most people buy products sight unseen, they rely on reviews and feedback. Therefore, it is natural for them to want to know what kind of experience others have had with your business. On websites, third party review collection services, such as Trustpilot[22] and Reviews.io[23], enable you to collect verified customer reviews. Most marketplaces collect customer feedback as an integral part of the aftersales process.

94% of consumers say an online review has convinced them to avoid a business. Furthermore, customers do not trust companies with less than 4/5 stars. 80% of consumers say the star ratings they trust the most are 4.0, 4.5 and 5 stars[24].

Maintaining a high feedback score is hard work. Unfortunately, many customers will leave a negative review before contacting the seller. Therefore, it is essential to monitor your reviews across all channels and resolve any negatives. If a negative cannot be resolved, you should

---

22   https://www.trustpilot.com

23   https://www.reviews.io

24   https://www.reviewtrackers.com/reports/online-reviews-survey

leave a comment. A few negatives are fine as people may think that a perfect score is fake.

Social media

Customers searching for your brand online will find your Social Media accounts alongside your website. By maintaining an active presence on the major Social Media networks, you can connect with customers and encourage them to follow you and share your posts. Active accounts with followers show that you are an established business.

Social media is covered in Chapter 8

Increasing average order value

Increasing average order value (AOV) will increase revenue and profit, all other things being equal. The figure used frequently involves the mean average of the order value:

AOV = Revenue / number of orders

The mean average is a valuable figure but can be misleading. It is often better to look at the modal average, i.e. the most common order value. For example, you may be selling a small number of high-value items, which skews the data. This is what happens on my nursery site, where a few high-ticket things (e.g. prams, room sets) push up the median AOV. The median average is the mid-point of a sorted list of orders.

Strategies for increasing AOV include:

- Offering free shipping over a certain threshold (e.g. spend £100, get free shipping).
- Discount over a certain point (e.g. spend £100, get £10 discount).

- Up-sell. Offering complimentary products to customers during their browsing journey or at checkout.

Free shipping is a common way to encourage customers to spend more. For example, putting your free shipping limit at 130% of your modal AOV will nudge customers to increase their basket size without spending too much more than they would normally. However, setting the threshold too high risks abandoned carts. An alternative option is to offer a discount for orders over a certain point, for example, a £10 or 10% discount for orders above £100.

Increasing order frequency

To state the obvious, the more often your customers buy from you, the more sales you will end up making over time. Therefore, order frequency is essential because a higher customer return rate means more revenue and lower acquisition cost. Maintaining a healthy order frequency is especially important to eCommerce businesses aiming to succeed in a saturated market.

Other reasons to focus on repeat customers include:

- **Repeat customers are likely to stay loyal.** Customers become increasingly more likely to buy from you again as their number of purchases increases. (source: Luxury Institute)[25]
- **Low hanging fruit.** It is 50% easier to sell to an existing customer than to a brand-new customer. (Source: Marketing Metrics)[26]

---

25   https://www.globenewswire.com/news-release/2016/10/19/1394364/0/en/Luxury-Client-Experience-Board-Reveals-How-Successful-Sales-Teams-Turn-First-Time-Shoppers-into-Long-Term-Clients.html

26   https://www.amazon.com/Marketing-Metrics-Definitive-Measuring-

- **They spend more on each purchase.** Returning customers have a higher average order value. (Source: Smile)[27]
- **Increases profits.** Increasing customer retention by 5% can increase profitability by 75%. (Source: Bain)[28]

Strategies for increasing order frequency

eCommerce companies use several techniques to increase order frequency:

- **Email marketing.** Encourage customers to join your email marketing list and receive regular offers.
- **Retargeting.** Specific adverts targeted at website visitors.
- **Subscriptions.** Subscriptions allow customers to sign up for regular deliveries of chosen items, with payment taken automatically.
- **Build trust and brand recognition** (see pages 8 and 14)
- **Loyalty scheme.** Reward loyal customers with money off e.g. get one point for every pound spent. Save 100 points and get £1 off the next purchase.
- **Offline marketing.** Include flyers in packaging that advertise offers.

Email marketing

Email marketing is one of the best ways to bring back customers, which is why eCommerce companies constantly strive to build their email list. 'Winback' emails are sent to re-engage with past customers. Most Winback email campaigns feature a series of emails sent over a few days to a few weeks.

Performance/dp/0137058292

27 https://blog.smile.io/calculate-average-order-value-and-5-tips-to-increase-it

28 https://hbswk.hbs.edu/archive/the-economics-of-e-loyalty

Email marketing is covered in Chapter 7.

Retargeting

Retargeting is where retailers serve ads to web browsers based on prior interaction with their business. Retargeting can take many forms, including site-based, search, display, social and email retargeting. The most common type of retargeting is site-based, where you serve ads to people who visited your website after they have left. These ads show up on many sites around the web, keeping your brand in front of your site visitors to encourage them to return.

Facebook and Google both offer retargeting ad campaigns and there are also specialist retargeting networks such as adroll.[29] So, for example, you can use Facebook to advertise to website visitors who added items to a basket but did not complete checkout.

Facebook and Google advertising, including retargeting, is covered in Chapters 8 and 5, respectively.

Subscriptions

Subscriptions are a great way to drive repeat traffic and generate regular income. If you sell consumable products, you can give your customers the option to pre-order a steady supply at a discount. Examples of companies offering subscriptions include contact lenses and coffee suppliers.

Another increasingly popular option is to offer a dedicated subscription box product. Examples include toy subscriptions for kids, clothing subscriptions and chocolate subscriptions.

---

[29]   https://www.adroll.com

Loyalty scheme

About 60-80% of customers who describe themselves as satisfied customers do not make a second purchase (Source: Bain)[30], so you must be proactive about enticing them back. Loyalty programs provide powerful motivation for buyers to create accounts and return to the site. A popular form of loyalty programme is to award points for purchases. Points can be exchanged for full or partial payment for an order. They also provide a reason to email customers to inform them of their unused points balance.

A rewards program can encourage your customers to increase their basket size and purchase more frequently. In addition, rewards motivate customers to come back to your store and stay away from competitors.

Offline marketing

Whilst beyond the scope of this book, offline marketing still plays a massive part in promoting any business, including online ones. Strategies to consider include:

- **Packaging inserts.** Include flyers in your packages that advertise new products and special offers.
- **Catalogues.** Though they are expensive to produce, people still respond to paper catalogues.
- **Magazine advertising.** A well-placed ad or insert can be highly effective if your target market coincides with a magazine's readership.
- **Print PR.** Getting your business into a popular magazine can affect sales enormously, especially if they also have an online version.

---

30   https://www.forbes.com/sites/larrymyler/2016/06/08/acquiring-new-customers-is-important-but-retaining-them-accelerates-profitable-growth/?sh=758f9d346671

Summary

Ecommerce businesses are identical to all other companies in that there are only three ways to grow their sales.

These are:

- Attract new prospects and convert them to customers.
- Increase the average transaction value.
- Encourage existing customers to order more frequently.

In each of these areas, you should investigate tactics for boosting performance. Even if you do not have the time, or resources, to work on these areas yourself, it is still essential that you understand the opportunities available, as this knowledge will enable you to manage others working on your behalf.

Finally, remember that retail is detail! To grow your eCommerce business, you need a good understanding of how it works as a business and the levers you can pull to improve performance.

Resources

The Total commerce platform Linnworks has compiled a list of all the major marketplaces in the world. These can be found here:

https://www.linnworks.com/whitepaper-access/complete-list-of-marketplaces

Of course, some marketplaces are much smaller than others and, from experience, only the largest are worth the effort. Webretailer has compiled a list of the largest marketplace by country:

https://www.webretailer.com/b/online-marketplaces/

The Department of International Trade in the UK has identified international marketplaces as a critical enabler for those UK businesses looking to sell overseas. As a result, they have compiled a valuable resource for trading internationally.

https://www.great.gov.uk/selling-online-overseas/

We cover the major international marketplaces in Chapter 11.

Google shopping can be used to drive traffic in nearly 100 countries worldwide.

https://support.google.com/merchants/answer/160637

To get the most out of our Google shopping, you should translate your site into the local language. If you have a small number of products, find a freelancer to do this on Upwork (www.upwork.com).

For larger catalogues, Google sheets have a translate function.

https://support.google.com/docs/answer/3093331?hl=en-GB

2:

IMPROVING BUSINESS PERFORMANCE

Turnover is vanity; profit is sanity. It is easy to be a busy fool in eCommerce. Downward price pressure is immense and I frequently liken online sales to a massive bun fight or a race to the bottom.

In this chapter, we talk about how to understand and improve the performance of your eCommerce business. This includes:

- **Margins.** The profitability of your business comes down to the margins you make when selling your products. In this chapter, you will learn about understanding and improving them.
- **Customer lifetime value.** By understanding the lifetime value of a customer, you know how much you can invest in acquiring each customer profitably.
- **Managing your inventory.** Having the best marketing in the world will not help you if you are selling the wrong product or permanently out of stock of the right ones.

Whatever the nature of your business, tracking your business performance allows you to understand your performance and make informed decisions. Is it going in the right direction? From where is your growth (or fall in sales) coming?

Understanding margins

A profit margin is the difference between what you sell an item for and what it costs. The higher the profit margin, the easier it will be for your business to grow and prosper. Margins vary widely by sector and by product type. For example, mark-ups in the fashion sector tend to be higher. However, these products have a high return rate and a short shelf life.

Gross Profit Margin

Gross margin is the most basic profit margin calculation. It can give a rough idea of the profitability of a product and it is helpful for a quick analysis of whether a product is worth stocking.

Gross Margin = (Product sale price – Product cost price) / Product sale price

Gross Margin gives a quick measure of the profitability of a product. For example, your business might decide to only stock items with a Gross profit of 50% or above.

Operating Profit Margin

The operating profit is the sales price of the product minus all the costs associated with the sale, i.e. the profit before overheads.

Operating Margin = (Product sale price – Product cost – Other costs) / Product sale price

Other costs could include:

- **Delivery.** There will inevitably be a delivery cost if you sell physical goods, whether you deliver yourself or the order is shipped directly by your supplier (drop-shipped).

- **Overheads.** You may wish to apportion a cost for overheads such as warehousing and staff. However, fixed costs are usually left out of this calculation.
- **Tax.** As Mark Twain said, 'in this world, nothing is certain except death and taxes'. There will be sales tax in most countries, ranging from 10 to 25%.
- **Payment.** Online payment services such as PayPal and Stripe charge between 1% and 4% for accepting payment by credit or debit card.
- **Marketing.** Marketing can be a fixed commission (e.g. Amazon, eBay) or variable (e.g. Google Ads charged by click).

The net operating margin should give you an accurate picture of how much money you make on each sale.

What is a good margin?

This is a question for your accountant or financial director! In my experience, in the UK, where VAT is 20%, branded products sell for about twice the cost price online. If you are sourcing your own products, you should be aiming for at least 3x cost price.

How to improve margins

Margins are tight in online retail and competition is fierce. So, take every opportunity you can to get a better price on materials. Here are some common strategies:

Ask!

I have frequently found that you can get discounts from suppliers simply by asking.

Go direct

Many retailers start off buying products from wholesalers. While buying multiple brands from the same supplier is convenient, buying directly from the manufacturer is often more cost-effective.

Buy in bulk

Usually, discounts are available for larger purchases. Deals can be on an order level (e.g. buy over £100 and get 10% off or at the product level (e.g. buy 25 and get a 5% discount). Increasing your order value may mean that you can order less frequently and increase the chances of stocking out.

Offer to pay more quickly

Suppliers value cash in the bank. Therefore, many suppliers will give a small discount if you offer to pay upfront, quickly or simply on time. Every little bit helps!

Cashback cards

Some business credit cards provide cashback of around 1%. If you pay off the card promptly, credit cards can provide working capital and additional time to pay. As the rate is punitive, only use credit cards if you have sufficient funds.

Own label products

Larger retailers (e.g. supermarkets) sell products under their own brand (e.g. Sainsbury's Baked Beans) to increase margins. However, with the rise of manufacturing in China, smaller retailers also have this option. We discuss options for own-label products below.

Sell internationally

In my experience, customers buying from overseas are less price sensitive. They are happy to pay the UK recommended retail price (RRP) + shipping.

Understanding the value of your customers

As mentioned in the previous chapter, it is cheaper and easier to sell to existing customers. Consequently, how many repeat customers your business gets is one measure of the health of your business. Your business should track how well you drive repeat business and constantly strive to improve your performance. High-performing companies will get as much as 40% of their sales through repeat customers. Ask yourselves the following questions:

- How often does it make sense for my customers to be purchasing? Remember that numbers will vary between sectors (e.g. consumables vs non-consumables).
- What might be stopping customers from purchasing more frequently?
- What can we do to encourage return customers?

Strategies for increasing repeat purchase rates are covered in Chapters 1 and 7. The following metrics are a good measure of how well a business retains customers:

Repeat Purchase Rate

Repeat purchase rate measures the number of customers who made more than one purchase in a designated period.

Repeat Purchase Rate = Number of customers who bought more than once / Total number of customers

This metric is best calculated over 3 to 12 months to give customers time to return.

Purchase Frequency

Purchase frequency is the number of times a typical customer purchases in a period.

Purchase frequency = Numbers of orders placed / Number of unique customers
(over 365 days).

Time between Purchases

The time between purchases shows you how often a typical customer goes before making a repeat purchase.

Time Between Purchases = Time / Purchase Frequency

Customer Lifetime Value

Acquiring a customer online usually requires some sort of marketing investment. Consequently, acquiring a new customer is more expensive than selling to an existing customer. Customer Lifetime Value measures how much a customer is worth to your business throughout their relationship with your brand.

Customer Lifetime Value = Customer Value × Average customer lifespan

Customer Value = Average purchase value / Average purchase frequency rate

Customer Lifetime Value is an excellent measurement of overall customer loyalty. You should improve your performance by increasing order frequency and average order value.

Cost Per Acquisition

Cost per Acquisition is the amount you typically spend to bring in a new customer. The acquisition cost calculation determines the value of a given promotional effort over a given period. For example, if a business spends £2500 to gain 250 new customers, the Cost per Acquisition is £10.

Acquisition Cost = Acquisition or promotional cost / Number of new customers

Your Customer Lifetime Value calculation decides the amount you are happy to spend on a new customer. It may be that you can lose money on the first order as you know that over the lifecycle of an average customer, they will be profitable.

Managing your inventory

Inventory is devilishly hard to manage. Too much and you tie up lots of money; too little and you miss out on sales.

Predicting how much you need on hand to fulfil orders is hard enough, but on top of this, you must contend with your supply chain. In my experience, suppliers are surprisingly slow at processing orders.

Optimising reordering

Getting stock at the right time is one of the biggest headaches in physical retail. If you do not have enough inventory, you risk running out of stock or 'stocking out' and missing sales. On the other hand, if you have too much stock, you will have money tied up in inventory that could be better used.

There are MBA-level courses on keeping the correct stock levels. However, if you are trying not to stock out when your supplier still has stock, then there are a few figures you need to record:

- Daily stock sales when in stock
- Time between orders
- Time to deliver.

Using this information, you can calculate your stock levels:

- **Reorder quantity.** *The daily sales × time between orders*
- **Minimum level.** The amount of stock needed to keep you in stock when you wait for an order to arrive is *daily sales × delivery time.*

This basic system assumes that the past is a guide to the future. It can also become seriously unstuck if stock levels of an item are low, e.g. if there is only one item in stock and this sells on the first day, the system will assume there will be one order every day.

Inventory metrics

Forecasting demand is essential for accurately predicting how much of a product you should purchase. Retailers lose $1.1 trillion globally from overstocks and out-of-stocks. (Source: Order Dynamics[31])

You will only know if your ordering system is working by measuring its performance.

So, monitor these simple inventory metrics to track the success of your ordering and adjust:

Sell-Through-Rate

Inventory sell-through rate measures the sales in relation to the amount they bought from a supplier. This metric is used to predict demand for a product and purchase the appropriate amount from suppliers.

Sell-Through-Rate (%) = (Number of units sold / Beginning inventory) × 100

---

31   https://www.retailwire.com/discussion/retailers-suffer-the-high-cost-of-overstocks-and-out-of-stocks

For example, if you start with 500 Gruffalo toys and sell 100, the toy's sell-through rate is 20%.

Sell-through rates help merchants know how efficiently they turn over their inventory and avoid costs related to storage or discounting. There are several ways you can improve sell-through, each with pros and cons.

- **Order less.** Rather than purchasing inventory based on instinct, research the popularity of a product before submitting a purchase order and use historical sales data (if available).
- **Order more frequently.** If your suppliers are reliable, you can order more regularly to top up your stock.
- **Launch a promotion.** Dropping prices will encourage sales but will result in lower profit margins.

Stock Turn

Stock turn (a.k.a. inventory turnover) is the number of times stock is sold through or used in a period. The higher the stock turn, the better because you sell a lot without stocking too much inventory.

Stock Turn = Cost of goods sold / Average inventory

For example, if your business' average inventory is £250,000 and the cost of goods sold in a year is £1,000,000, the stock turn is 4.0.

Product performance

Most eCommerce businesses have hundreds if not thousands of products for sale. The 'Pareto Principle' (or 80/20 rule) holds in many companies. This principle states that 80% of sales will come from 20% of products. If this is the case in your business, you should watch your top sellers like a hawk and ensure they are always in stock. Conversely, you should also monitor products that are selling poorly as these are taking up space and money which might be better spent on other things.

I recommend having a rolling programme for analysing the bottom 10% of your inventory. Check that there are no easily identifiable reasons why each product is not selling (e.g. incorrect price or not live). If no reason can be found, be ruthless!

Lost Sales

A measure of lost sales is an excellent way to gauge if you are trying to run too lean on inventory, especially for top-selling products.

Lost Sales = Days out of stock × Average daily sales

Smarter buying

Products are at the heart of every eCommerce business. Your product selection can make or break your business. This section discusses the different strategies used in eCommerce to source and deliver products. Using a mix of strategies can increase your range, improve margins and increase sales.

There are several ways to source and deliver your products:

- **Branded products.** Off-the-shelf products bought from suppliers.
- **Own Label products.** Developing a product can be lucrative but is also time-consuming and risky. As the brand owner, you will be responsible for product safety.

- **White label products.** A shortcut to developing a product is to buy an off-the-shelf product from an overseas manufacturer and put your branding on it. This practice is known as white labelling. As the brand owner, you will be responsible for product safety.
- **Dropship.** Dropshipping is where the manufacturer delivers directly to the end customer.

Branded products

Branded products are products made by product manufacturers that they sell wholesale. These companies will typically sell wholesale to retailers, who then sell directly to consumers. Increasingly, brands are selling directly, but most well-known brands still depend on their retailers.

Pros: These are products bought off-the-shelf, so they are easy to source. If the brand is well known, your business will pick up on the demand they generate through their marketing activities. Many products are available from 'wholesalers' who will sell a range of products which can be purchased together. This allows the purchase of small qualities of any individual product.

Cons: It is unlikely you will be the only seller for any barcoded product unless you have managed to enter an exclusive arrangement with the manufacturer. Therefore, margins are likely to be low, as sellers compete for business on price.

Own label products

Designing products from scratch is not as hard as it used to be as factories in China manufacture in small batches, keeping your inventory risk low. In addition, product design and packaging expertise are available, at low cost, from professional services marketplaces such as Upwork.com[32].

---

32   https://www.upwork.com

Pros: Margins will be much higher for your own branded products as you will be the only seller. This additional margin can be taken or spent on advertising to build the brand.

Cons: You will be responsible for the manufacture of these products and the product certifications needed. Typically, the manufacture will occur in the Far East, which adds complications such as language and delivery delays.

Minimum order volume will be much higher than for branded products, typically several hundred units at a time. In addition, as items ship from overseas, the lead time to delivery will also be weeks or months. Finally, as the brand will be new, you will need to build up brand recognition from scratch.

'White-labelled' products

White labelled products are halfway between developing a brand and buying products off the shelf. Through product sourcing sites, such as Alibaba[33], it is possible to source an unimaginably vast range of ready-made products from Chinese factories. These products are unbranded but can have a brand added to differentiate them. These are known as 'white-labelled' or 'private-labelled' products.

Pros: Offer your own branded products without the hassle of designing them from scratch. White labelling is widespread and is used by many major brands. For example, I have been to Ikea and seen them stocking a product I sold under an entirely different brand.

Cons: White-labelled products will not be as differentiated as products designed from scratch and several sellers may sell the same product under a different brand. Products must be fully compliant with local safety standards.

---

33   https://www.alibaba.com

Dropshipping

Dropshipping is where a retailer makes a sale, but the supplier ships a product directly to the customer without the retailer touching it.

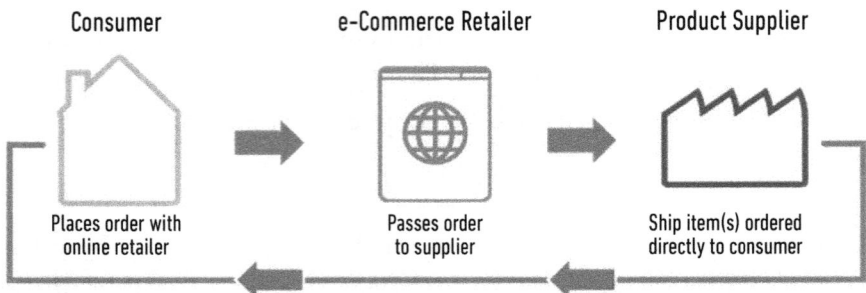

Consumer	e-Commerce Retailer	Product Supplier
Places order with online retailer	Passes order to supplier	Ship item(s) ordered directly to consumer

Fig. 2. The dropshipping process

Dropshipping is very appealing as the retailer takes no inventory risk. Dropshipping is, in many ways, the holy grail of eCommerce. There is a lot written online about it being the path to riches, but it is fraught with difficulties:

- **Control of delivery experience.** If you are dropshipping items, your delivery experience will only be as good as your supplier. Consequently, the quality of delivery varies considerably.
- **Delivery times.** For items dropshipped from overseas, the delivery period is several weeks.
- **Quality of data.** Many suppliers will offer dropshipping, but only a few will be good at it. Typically, a supplier will only update their stock levels once a week, so the retailer will often make sales they cannot fulfil.
- **Returns.** Returns will generally go directly to the retailer. These will build up over time.
- **Shipping costs.** Dropshippers will typically charge a higher shipping cost than a retailer's own. For example, a Royal Mail parcel costs £3 to ship in the UK, while drop shippers may charge £4-5.

- **Low quality.** Major brands and suppliers do not typically dropship. Consequently, products available for dropship tend to be low quality and unbranded.
- **Low margins.** As dropshippers will offer their service to anyone, the competition is high and margins low.

If you can make dropshipping work, great! However, it usually does not work as smoothly as advertised. Bear in mind that the margin for error on channels like Amazon is < 1%, i.e. if your order defect rate is > 1%, your account can be closed. If your dropship partner only delivers 95% of products on time, you ask for trouble.

Holding stock ties up capital and requires storage space and staff to fulfil. However, you are entirely in control of the end-to-end fulfilment experience.

Retail arbitrage

Retail arbitrage is where retailers re-sell products from other retailers, adding their mark-up. This has the advantage of not requiring any stock. However, margins will be paper thin and opportunities transitory. You also depend on an unsuspecting third party to manage your delivery. Not to be recommended.

What is the right product mix?

As we have seen, all the strategies have their advantages and dis-advantages. But, as usual, using a mixed approach has advantages:

- **Branded.** If you are a manufacturer, consider selling other people's products in your store to expand your range quickly.
- **White label.** Retailers can improve their margins by developing their own range of products.
- **Dropshipping.** Increase your range for little cost and try out new sectors. Particularly useful for large bulky items.

Product Research

Predicting what products will sell is a challenging task. Thankfully, several data sources are available when researching a marketplace and identifying opportunities.

Search queries

You can establish market trends and popular products by looking for popular and trending keyword searches. Some free products provide keyword volumes:

- **Google Trends.**[34] Shows trending searches around the world.
- **Google Keyword Planner.**[35] Provides search term volume for Google Ads customers.
- Amazon search volume. **Sonar**[36] is a free Amazon keyword research tool from Sellics.

Browse popular products on online marketplaces

Published market research from companies such as Mintel[37] is costly. However, online marketplaces, such as Amazon, list best-selling items to inform purchasing decisions. Sources of information include:

- **Amazon best sellers** (UK[38] and US[39])
- **Amazon sales rank.** Amazon product pages state a 'Best Sellers Rank' which shows how popular an item is in its category.

---

34   https://trends.google.com/trends/?geo=US
35   https://ads.google.com/intl/en_uk/home/tools/keyword-planner
36   https://sellics.com/sonar-amazon-keyword-tool
37   https://www.mintel.com
38   https://www.amazon.co.uk/Best-Sellers-Welcome/zgbs
39   https://www.amazon.com/Best-Sellers/zgbs

- **eBay research.** eBay's Terapeak[40] tool will give the best sellers for a given category.
- **Google Shopping.** Google's Best Sellers[41] report lists popular products and brands on their Google shopping ads program.
- **Amazon research tools.** Products such as Jungle Scout[42] and Bqool[43] provide a suite of tools for interrogating Amazon sales history to find product opportunities.

Other sources of product data

- **Media.** Investigate the products which are advertised on major websites and in print media.
- **Competition.** What are the websites of the biggest retailers promoting?
- **High street stores.** Take a trip to a local store to see their inventory on display

Looking for product opportunities

If you are researching products to buy or make, tools like Jungle Scout and Bqool will enable you to query the Amazon marketplace. Using these tools, you can analyse where there is demand and limited supply or weak competition:

- **Low reviews.** It is hard to compete with a listing that has many reviews as these will hog the top spot in the Amazon search. So, one strategy is to find products with good sales but few reviews and create competing products.

---

40 https://www.ebay.co.uk/help/selling/selling-tools/terapeak-research?id=4853

41 https://support.google.com/merchants/answer/9488679

42 https://junglescout.grsm.io/vendlab1348

43 http://affiliate.bqool.com/idevaffiliate.php?id=780

- **Non-optimised listings.** Find poorly optimised products (short descriptions, low-quality images, few reviews) with good revenue (established using tools such as Jungle Scout) and create competitor products. The higher-quality content should compete with this product and eventually outrank it.
- **Few searches returned.** Look at keyword demand on Amazon and find niches with lots of searches but few or poorly matched results.

Your product should appeal to a specific, enthusiastic audience. Identifying and serving a niche will help build brand awareness and drive traffic from new and returning customers.

Assess product viability

So, you have done your product research and decided to venture into making your range of products. Manufacturing a product sounds like a daunting task. However, we now live in a global economy where you can quickly get hold of manufacturers all over the world. Furthermore, the costs of developing a product and the minimum order quantities are not as high as you might think.

eBay and Amazon's algorithms reward established products and sellers with great reviews and a long sales history. Getting the top spot in search can mean the difference between success and failure. If your product competes in a space with well-established brands, it may not be easy to make any headway. Instead, try and find a niche in a new market where there is room for innovation and new businesses.

Below are some tips for choosing a winning product.

Solves a problem for an identifiable market

Do your research and know the target customer for your product. If your product does not address a need in the market, it will not sell. It is best to create a product in an area about which you are passionate. When brainstorming for ideas, reflect on problems in your life for inspiration.

Sturdy

Remember that your product will be thrown around a warehouse and enter that maelstrom known as the postal service. If it is not a solid product, then it stands a good chance of never making it to the end customer in one piece. For example, I once ordered from a website that sold lightbulbs online – only one of the four products I bought arrived intact. Not a good business to be in!

Good quality

The higher the quality of your product, the more you can charge for it and the greater your customer's satisfaction. Unfortunately, you will need to sell a mountain of cheap junk to make any money and your customers will be upset when it breaks.

Healthy margin

If you are going to make a product and invest in the stock, make sure you get a healthy margin.

Lightweight and compact

If your product is bulky and heavy, it will be expensive to ship from the manufacturer to the customer. Also, if you run a warehouse, bigger items will take up more valuable space.

Product lifespan

Selling a consumable or disposable product is often a wise choice from a business perspective as it encourages repeat sales. Another option is a subscription box business model, in which your customer signs up for monthly deliveries and payments.

In my local street market, a man sells super-hot sauce. I bought one bottle several years ago and I have not finished it! Offering a product with recurring demand will lower your marketing costs and increase your average customer lifetime value.

Seasonality

When making purchasing decisions, consider seasonality. For example, if you are in the outdoor equipment business, you will be very busy in the summer but much quieter in winter. Seasonality is a challenge. However, there are ways of mitigating the risk, including running promotions and shipping internationally.

Whether or not your range is seasonal, seasonality affects revenue for all online stores. Almost all businesses see sales rise in the last quarter of the year and events like Black Friday and Cyber Monday get bigger every year.

Finding a manufacturer

Once you have decided on the product or type of product you wish to source, you need to find a manufacturer. You can access an enormous range of factories in the Far East through sites such as Alibaba, where manufacturing costs are much lower. When researching business partners, be sure to ask the following questions.

- What is their capacity? Can they scale up as your demand grows?
- What will the total cost of production and shipping be? Are there any hidden fees?
- How long will it take to create, fulfil and ship the product?
- What are their business terms?
- Who is responsible for the product specification?
- What are the minimum order quantities?

- How much will the carriage cost?
- What is their feedback? On sourcing sites like Alibaba, you will see feedback from past customers.
- Supply chain. Consumers are becoming more interested in where their products are from. Ask about the conditions under which the product is made and where they source their supplies.
- Dispute process. What is the process if you are not happy with the delivery? Sites like Alibaba do have a dispute process, but you should not rely on this. Paying by credit cards will give additional protection.

Before committing to purchase in bulk, insist on a sample to ensure that the products meet your expectations.

Summary

Without understanding and tracking your business performance, you will not have a clear picture of how well your business is performing and of the progress it is making. Margins are tight in eCommerce and it is easy to lose money on sales without realising it! Hiring an external accountant is expensive but can help impose financial rigour on the business.

An eCommerce entrepreneur must excel at the eCommerce part of their business and at the more conventional retail activities of choosing products, setting prices and managing stock. If you do not have the right quantities of the right products, your online business will not thrive.

Purchasing the right products is a core eCommerce activity. These will preferably sell at a high margin and in large volumes! There are multiple ways to source stock and your company, like major retailers, will probably be most successful if you use them in combination. Consumers will be looking for major brands but also drawn to cheaper own-label goods. Dropshipping is an excellent way of expanding your range at a low cost.

Remember that companies are generally valued not on turnover but a profit multiple, starting from around four times your annual profits. So, for example, if your company makes £250,000 a year, it will sell for upwards of £1 million. Therefore, a more profitable company is a more significant nest egg or will provide more funds for your next venture. Profit can be improved with a laser focus on margins and advertising costs. By choosing desirable products with good profit potential, you will encourage repeat business, reducing your cost of sale. Careful product selection can turn a struggling business into a thriving one while at the same time giving you more funds to invest and grow your business or to pay yourself more.

PART II:

INCREASING WEBSITE SALES

Having a website has massive advantages. It gives complete control over the online experience you offer to your customers. In addition, having a website allows you to use a broader range of online marketing techniques. You can use these to drive customers to your business and help you understand their behaviour.

However, websites are not the only way to sell online. The appeal of marketplaces such as Amazon is growing as they offer every product under the sun and easy payment options. In addition, services such as Shopify are fast commoditising the process of selling online, increasing competition and making it more difficult for sellers to stand out.

I've always found selling on a website much harder than on marketplaces. This is because commissions are mostly fixed on marketplaces, whereas website advertising is mainly charged on a pay-per-click basis. That said, get your website right and the potential to encourage return customers (not possible on marketplaces) means higher margins and a more sustainable business.

In addition, by selling through a website, you are in complete control of your marketing. You can:

- Build an email list to broadcast offers and entice back previous customers.
- Use retargeting and abandoned cart emails to entice people back to your site.
- Use Social Media to form connections with customers.
- Drive traffic to your site using paid advertising on Google and Facebook.
- Optimise the performance of your website to turn it into a selling machine!

None of these options are open to you if you sell on marketplaces as you depend on the platform to drive traffic to your listings. You can drive traffic to your marketplace listings, but that is not advisable as you still must pay the commission on the sale. Drive the same traffic to your website and there is no commission!

In Part 2, we look at techniques for driving traffic to your website (Search Engine Optimisation, Paid Search, Social Media, Email Marketing and Affiliate Marketing) and how to measure and improve the performance of your website in converting this traffic into customers.

3:

IMPROVING WEBSITE PERFORMANCE

Although services, such as Shopify, are standardising the process of selling online, website owners still have plenty of opportunities to personalise the experience they offer their customers and get the most out of their marketing activities.

This chapter looks at building a successful eCommerce site, measuring your website performance (website analytics), and using this information to maximise your website's sales.

What makes a good website?

It is not possible to fully spec out a website here. However, here is an (incomplete) list of functionalities that all good eCommerce websites should feature. Performing well in these areas will increase website traffic, improve conversion rate and lead to more sales.

Site speed

Site speed has a massive effect on the conversion rate and you should aim to maximise your website performance. Website conversion rate decreases by an average of 4.42% with each extra second of load time (between seconds 0-5) (Source: Portent[44]). Furthermore, Google[45] has found that 53% of visits are abandoned if a mobile site takes longer than three seconds to load.

Your site's speed also affects your natural search engine performance, with Google using site performance as a significant ranking factor. Google's Search Console[46] tool benchmarks every site against 'Core Web Vitals'. Core Web Vitals are a ranking factor in its search algorithm (Source: Moz[47]).

Search Engine (SEO) friendly

As we will discuss in Chapter 4, natural search traffic is a significant source of customers. However, eCommerce sites differ in how easy they are to configure in a search engines friendly way. Platforms provide different support levels for important SEO features like Robot. txt file, XML sitemaps and metadata (covered in Chapter 4 on SEO). Also, hosted platforms, like Shopify, allow no access to the hosting environment and site architecture, although these are some of the most significant ranking factors.

Mobile friendly

Over 50% of internet traffic now occurs on a mobile device (source: Statcounter[48]). So, your site's mobile friendliness should be a primary consideration when choosing a platform and a website template. With a responsive website, content adapts to the device and its screen "real estate" and adjusts to provide the most user-friendly experience.

---

44 https://www.portent.com/blog/analytics/research-site-speed-hurting-everyones-revenue.htm

45 https://www.thinkwithgoogle.com/intl/en-gb/marketing-strategies/app-and-mobile/mobile-page-speed-new-industry-benchmarks

46 https://search.google.com/search-console/about

47 https://moz.com/blog/core-web-vitals

48 https://gs.statcounter.com/platform-market-share/desktop-mobile-tablet

High-resolution images (> 300 Pixels per inch)

Shoppers want to see multiple product images and lifestyle shots of the product in use. Studies have shown that bigger, higher quality, zoomable images increase the conversion rate (source: VWO[49]). Furthermore, having more than one image doubles the conversion rate (source: eBay Labs[50]). However, be careful not to overdo image size as larger images are slower to load.

High-quality product descriptions

Writing comprehensive product descriptions is vital to eCommerce success, but unfortunately, suppliers are not always helpful. Persevere as quality product descriptions will benefit your business in several ways:

- **Conversion rate.** Quality descriptions that sell a product will boost the conversion rate.
- **Search engine traffic.** Unique product descriptions will drive more natural (a.k.a. free or organic) search traffic from Google's search engine.
- **Google shopping traffic.** If you are using Google's shopping ads program, high-quality product descriptions will drive more paid and free impressions.
- **Social media.** High-quality product descriptions are more likely to be shared on Social Media platforms.

User-friendly

Your website should be a pleasure to use and convert browsers into buyers. About 76% of users say ease of use is the most important characteristic of a website (Source: HubSpot[51]). Your website should

---

49   https://vwo.com/success-stories/optimics

50   http://citeseerx.ist.psu.edu/viewdoc/download?doi=10.1.1.648.6208&rep=rep1&type=pdf

51   https://blog.hubspot.com/blog/tabid/6307/bid/14953/what-do-76-of-consumers-want-from-your-website-new-data.aspx

help shoppers find what they want quickly and provide a seamless checkout experience. To improve the usability of your site, consider the following:

- **Categorisation.** Take care to organise your products into a simple, logical structure.
- **Checkout.** The checkout process should be short (preferably one page) with a clear indication of progress and no surprises e.g. additional costs. The checkout page is especially important for optimising conversions and reducing cart abandonment.
- **Guest checkout.** Forcing customers to create an account will put off some people.
- **Shipping cost.** Shipping rates and delivery times should be clearly stated early in the buying process.
- **Site search.** Site search is a popular website feature but often performs poorly.
- **Related items.** Showing users other products will increase basket size and average order value.

Compelling landing pages

The page where a user enters your site is the landing page. If the user is directed to this page by an advert (e.g. Google shopping) or from a Google natural search result, the quality of this page will be vital in converting them from a browser into a customer. Landing pages need to perform several functions on the site:

- **Inform.** The page should contain well-written and helpful information on their topic. For example, category pages should be constructed so that each category has a full page of products and a good description.
- **Convert.** Your product pages will be landing pages for specific product-related searches. These pages should contain

compelling copy, images to sell the product and a clear call to action.
- **Drive natural search traffic.** Carefully write pages so they contain search terms that browsers use to find products. This is known as search engine optimisation and is covered in Chapter 4.

For more information on landing pages, see Chapter 5 on Paid Search.

Internationalisation

More commerce business is occurring internationally and the strongest growing markets are outside the West. It is becoming easier to sell to these markets through your website as advertising platforms such as Google Ads work worldwide. For example, Google Shopping now operates in 94 countries[52], accessible from a single Google account.

International sales are a significant opportunity for your business and shipping to the major markets (Europe, North America, Japan, Australasia) is straightforward. You will get some sales by offering international shipping options and having your site in English and your local currency. However, the conversion rate will be improved by localising your site to the users' language and currency.

Multiple payment methods

Providing choice on payments is about appealing to as many customer preferences as possible and ensuring that people do not abandon purchases because they cannot pay in the way they want. Research has shown that 6% of shoppers had abandoned carts due to a lack of payment options (source: Salescycle[53]). Credit/Debit cards are the

---

52 https://support.google.com/merchants/answer/160637?hl=en-GB#zippy=

53 https://www.salecycle.com/blog/strategies/infographic-people-abandon-shopping-carts

most popular but other payment forms, such as PayPal, come in a close second.

User-generated reviews and feedback

Rating services such as Trustpilot, Feefo and Reviews.io have become ubiquitous and 57% of consumers will only use a business with a rating of four or more stars (Source: Brightlocal[54]). User-generated content, such as product reviews, provide 'Social Proof' of a business' reliability. Having some negative reviews can often be positive. Products with no negative reviews are seen as censored and shoppers will assume the positive reviews are fake.

Understanding your website's performance

So how do you measure how well your website is performing in attracting browsers and converting them into buyers? There is a range of primary and more advanced metrics that website owners can use to help them understand how well their site is performing.

Basic web metrics

These basic web performance metrics make up the basic building blocks of understanding what users are doing on your website and they can be combined to create more advanced metrics (see below). The resources section at the end of this chapter links to benchmarking metrics.

Sessions

A session is a period of user activity on a website. For example, a user may come to your site, browse some pages, and purchase. If they are inactive for 30 minutes, the session ends.

---

54   https://www.brightlocal.com/research/local-consumer-review-survey

Note that a second session is recorded if the user returns later that day.

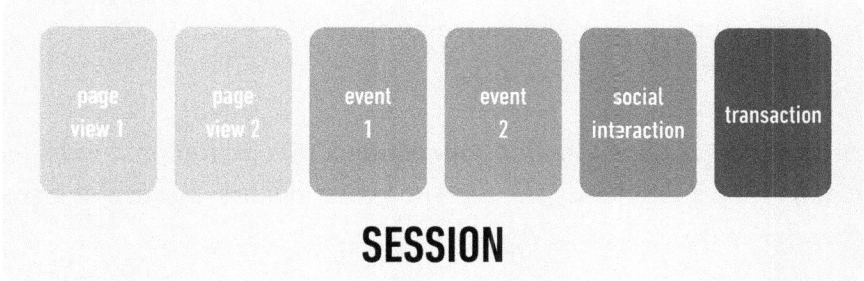

Fig. 3. Example session

Users

This is the number of visitors, within a given period, spending at least one session on your website. A visitor returning twice will be recorded as one user.

Pageviews

The number of pages visited on your site in each period.

Pages per session

The average pages viewed during a session on your website are calculated as page views divided by sessions. More pages per session mean that users are more engaged and visit more of your site.

Average session duration

The average duration of visitors' sessions. Longer sessions indicate more-engaged visitors.

Bounce rate

Bounce rate is the percentage of visits where users viewed only one page and left. A high bounce rate suggests that people leave your site because they are not finding the item they seek. You can minimise bounce rates by ensuring that landing pages are relevant to the advertising campaigns that referred them to your site.

Percentage of new sessions

The percentage of new visitors to your website. A successful website will have a mix of new and returning visitors.

Conversion

A conversion (a.k.a. Goal) is completing a user action on a website, e.g. making a purchase. The website owner defines conversion types that they wish to track.

Advanced website metrics: web analytics

Beyond these basic metrics, a deeper understanding of the users on your site can be obtained by tracking their behaviour as they use your site. Web Analytics is the measurement and analysis of visitors' behaviour on a website. It gives website owners vital information on who is visiting and what they are doing. If appropriately managed, this information can inform marketing activities and website design, which leads to increased traffic and higher sales. Many businesses, however, do not measure the performance of their website in even the most basic sense.

Web Analytics can tell merchants:

- **Who their customers are?** For example, where are they from? What are their demographics? This information can be used to create more targeted campaigns and offers.
- **How did they find your business?** The referring source will be recorded, e.g. referring site, search engine, Social Media platform. This information will help you understand which source refers the most traffic and is the most profitable.
- **What do they do when they get to your website?** By analysing customer behaviour, you can change your site to improve the number of browsers who purchase (the conversion rate).

Businesses can choose the Key Performance Indicators (KPIs) against which to measure their website's performance from these metrics. These are the metrics that most impact the bottom line of your business. Popular KPIs include sales, conversion rate and average order value.

Website Analytics can help an eCommerce website improve in three principal areas:

Online promotion

As covered in this book, many different methods are available for promoting a website. Web Analytics can help identify which ones work best for your business by measuring and comparing sales channels. The data collected can help answer several questions about your marketing:

- Which marketing channels refer visitors to your site?
- How much traffic do they drive?
- What products do customers buy?
- How much do customers spend?
- Where do your site visitors live?
- What are the demographics of your audience?
- What is the conversion by channel?

The answers to these questions will enable you to focus your marketing efforts, showing you the channels to invest in and which to abandon. They can also help you define and understand your target audience.

Website design and performance

Online promotion, such as Paid Search or Search Engine Optimisation, gets people to a site, but it is what they do when they get there that matters. A website's navigation and usability can have a massive effect on its performance. Installing tracking software, such as Google Analytics allows the analysis of user navigation paths through the website. This highlights usability issues.

Insights include:

- **Exit points.** Are users leaving the site at particular points before completing a conversion e.g. when shipping is quoted?
- **Shopping cart abandonment.** What percentage of your items are added to a cart but never bought?
- **Bounce rates.** The percentage of website visitors who leave the site after viewing only one page. A high bounce rate indicates that the site does not meet user expectations.
- **Page traffic.** Which pages on your site get the most traffic?
- **Site speed.** How quickly do your pages load?

These insights give you concrete ways of improving your site performance. For example, you could learn that certain products get lots of traffic but few conversions. By enhancing page elements (e.g. description, images and prices), you can run comparative tests to learn which features improve performance.

Search Engine Optimisation (SEO)

Insights from web analytical tools also provide valuable pointers for improving your search engine optimisation. For example, they can help answer questions about how users find and interact with your site, including:

- How much traffic is from natural search?
- Which landing pages get the most traffic?
- Popular search queries that drive traffic to your site.

Using this information, you can see what content on your site attracts search engine traffic and the keywords driving traffic. You can use this information to discover where you underperform so you can create higher quality content.

Key Performance Indicators (KPIs)

Web analytics takes the speculation out of running a website. For example, you can tell how much revenue a particular campaign, channel or promotion generates. However, understanding your website's performance requires identifying key performance indicators (KPIs) that affect its performance.

KPIs help inform website optimisation and the direction of your overall business strategy. If you are trying to decide which metrics are the most important to track for your business, consider:

- If this metric changed, what impact would it have on the company?
- Will improving this metric help us reach our strategic goals? What is it that your website is trying to achieve?
- Will improving this metric also improve other metrics? For example, improving the conversion rate will also improve the cost per conversion.

Some of the key metrics you should consider for your business's KPIs are listed below.

Conversion rate

A conversion can take different forms, depending on the purpose of a website. On most retail websites, a conversion is usually a sale. Conversion rate is the number of conversions (i.e. visitors taking the action you wanted them to take) divided by the total number of visitors.

Conversion rate (%) = (completed conversions / number of visitors) × 100

A better conversion rate can dramatically affect the profitability of your site. According to Wordstream,[55] the average conversion rate is 2.35%, but some businesses achieve above 10%. A healthy conversion rate means you have an engaged customer base and is a sign of growth and success. It is the mark of a quality website.

Cost Per Conversion

The Cost per Conversion can compare the price of different types of advertising or promotion. The metric focuses on results and not simply costs. A campaign may have a high absolute cost but a low cost per conversion, making it a cost-effective campaign. Conversely, a second campaign may have a limited budget but a high cost per conversion, making it expensive.

Cost Per Conversion = Costs / Number of sales

Average Order Value (AOV)

The Average Order Value measures how much your customers typically spend on a single order. Hopefully, when people visit your website, they buy more than one item or choose more expensive or higher-margin products. The average order value measures the success of cross-selling tactics on the website.

Average Order Value = Total order value / Number of orders

Shopping Cart Abandonment

Shopping cart abandonment refers to users adding items to their shopping basket but leaving the site without paying for the goods.

---

55   https://www.wordstream.com/blog/ws/2014/03/17/what-is-a-good-conversion-rate

This is a widespread occurrence online, with some websites reporting as much as 50% of shopping carts abandoned.

Shopping Cart Abandonment (%) = (Number of completed carts / Carts started) × 100

Abandonment happens for a variety of reasons. Users may be bored with the number of screens in the shopping checkout or just visit the checkout to find the shipping costs. Many of the reasons for checkout abandonment lie in poor usability and navigation.

You should monitor your abandonment rates and use your analytics tool to see where customers are lost. By optimising this part of the process, you can reduce the percentage of dropouts. This will improve the return on investment from online advertising and increase sales without increasing spending.

Return on Investment (ROI)

Return on investment is a metric used to measure an investment's effectiveness, be it a new computer system or online marketing campaign.

Return on Investment % (ROI) = (Return / Investment) × 100

For example, an online electronics seller creates a PPC campaign to sell iPads. Each sale of an iPad generates a profit of £50. The PPC campaign costs £2000 and makes 200 sales.

Return on Investment = (200/2000) × 100 = 500%

Web Analytics software

Measuring a website's performance requires the use of Web Analytics software. This software takes the basic information from server log files and transforms it into readable reports. Web Analytics packages are easy to use, quick to install and cheap. The most popular Web Analytics package is Google Analytics,[56] a powerful, free tool from Google.

Implementing tracking

Web analytics software uses JavaScript code to gather website usage data. The code is added to all site pages and places a cookie in the browser of every site visitor. The cookie then sends a 'hit' to Google Analytics that reports each user's interaction with your site.

A simple setup will track page views, visitors, pages per visit and visitor location. However, tracking more exciting metrics such as cost-per-conversion will require additional coding.

Type of hits tracked by Web Analytics

Web Analytics systems record three types of hits:

- **Page View hit.** This hit is sent each time someone visits a page on a site. It contains information, including the device used, browser type and pages visited.
- **Event hit.** Sent when a visitor acts on a site, for example filling in a form, clicking a link or playing a video.
- **Transaction/eCommerce hit.** Sent when a site visitor makes a purchase. It includes detailed insights such as the products bought and the amount spent.

---

56   https://analytics.google.com

Google Analytics

Google Analytics is Google's free web analytics package and has become the industry standard. It is hugely powerful, supplying website owners with many website metrics.

Fig. 4. Google Analytics dashboard

Google Analytics does not just collect data from your site. It also generates reports to display that data intelligently. These reports give critical insight into your site and the people who visit it. Google Analytics contains a wealth of built-in reports which help you understand your website performance. You can also build your reports or segment built-in reports to drill down on performance.

Real-time reports

Real-Time reports allow you to watch activity as it happens on your site. The reports are updated continuously and each hit is recorded just after it occurs. For example, you can see how many people are on your site currently, the pages or events with which they are interacting and which goal conversions have occurred. Reports include:

- **Locations.** The geographic location of your active users.
- **Traffic Sources.** The sources that referred the users who are on your site right now.

- **Content.** Pages viewed during the past 30 minutes.
- **Conversions.** Real-time goal completions.

Audience reports

Audience reports give details about your visitors and their behaviour.

- **Demographics.** Age and gender.
- **Interests.** For example, shopping, food or fashion.
- **Location.** Where visitors are located.
- **Language.** Language spoken.
- **Behaviour.** How often do these visitors come to your website?
- **Technology and Mobile.** The technology used to view your website, e.g. browser type.

Acquisition reports

These reports give information on the traffic sources (channels) that drove traffic and visitor behaviour by channel.

- **Traffic sources.** e.g. paid search, natural search, referral.
- **Google Ads.** Data from a connected Google Ads account.
- **Search console.** Data from a connected Google Search console related to your natural search performance.
- **Social.** Traffic from social networks.

Merchants can drill down for each channel to see metrics such as bounce rate, pages per visit, revenue and conversions.

Behaviour reports

Behaviour reports tell you about the performance of the content on your site.

- **Most popular** pages on your site.
- **Landing pages.** Most popular entry pages on your website.
- **Exit pages.** Most common points of exit.

- **Site search terms.** Top search terms from internal site search.
- **Site speed.** How fast your website loads.

Conversions

These reports measure how well your site encourages users to meet predefined goals (or conversions). These can be events such as signing up for a newsletter or purchasing.

Goals

The Goals report summarises your goals, including the number of completions and the conversion rate for each. Goals are user-defined actions you want to track. You can set micro and macro goals to understand what activities contribute to overall outcomes. For example, the various stages of the checkout process could be micro goals towards the macro goal of making a sale.

For your goals, you will be able to track the following metrics:

- **Goal Completions.** The total number of conversions.
- **Goal Value.** The monetary value of conversions.
- **Goal-conversion Rate.** The rate of conversions across all sessions.
- **Abandonment Rate.** The people who did not complete your step-by-step goal/number of people who started towards your goal.

Ecommerce

The Ecommerce reports enable you to drill down on your sales to understand which products and promotions drive performance.

- **Product Performance.** Product-level sales data.
- **Sales Performance.** Transaction-level data.
- **Marketing.** Performance of promotions and coupons.

You must add the eCommerce code to the pages of your site to access this data. This is a special piece of tracking code that sends additional transaction-level data to Google Analytics[57].

Multi-channel funnels

The customer journey to your website may often be via an indirect route. For example, they may interact with your business on various other sites before purchasing. Alternatively, they may click on a paid search advert and go to a cashback site before buying.

The Multi-Channel Funnel report investigates how different channels feed into your funnel. This includes:

- **Assisted Conversions.** Where a channel was on the conversion path but was not the last step.
- **Top Conversion Paths.** The top routes to conversion, e.g. Paid Search > Organic Search.
- **Path Length.** The number of interactions in a path.

Funnels

A user may pass through several intermediary pages to reach a conversion goal on a website, e.g. completing checkout or registration. A funnel is a graphical way of displaying the dropout rates over the series of pages through which the user must navigate to reach the goal.

---

57   https://developers.google.com/analytics/devguides/collection/analyticsjs/
ecommerce

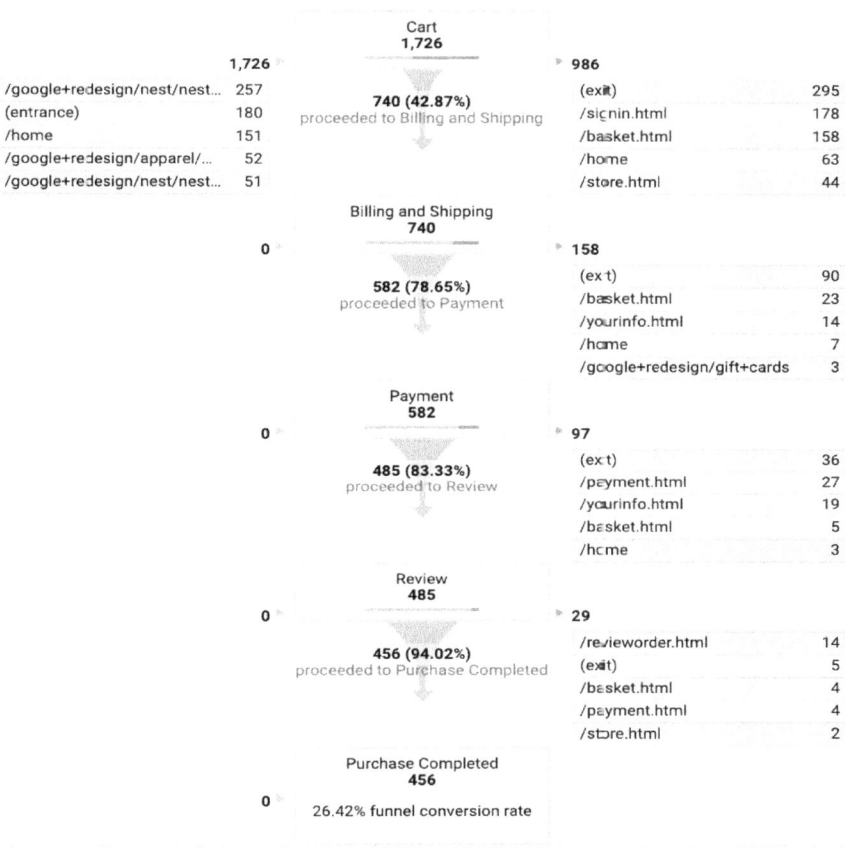

Fig. 5. Funnel visualisation

The purpose of funnels is to see how efficiently your pages direct visitors to your goal. It allows a website owner to see how users leave the site and make the necessary changes to improve the conversion rate. If any page in a conversion funnel is overly complicated or not designed to be user-friendly, you will see a significant drop-off.

Over 50% of users do not continue from the Cart to Billing and Shipping steps in the example above. By redesigning this process, the website could significantly improve its sales without spending more money on advertising.

Filtering and segmenting data

Removing irrelevant data by filtering

Your reports are only as reliable as the underlying data, so it is essential to ensure that they include only valid data. You might, for instance, wish to exclude visitors to your website from within your organisation.

Filters can remove information from your web analytics reports by excluding visits from particular locations (defined by IP address). You could find, for example, that you receive visits from a location that never convert. This could be a bot and your metrics will be more accurate by excluding this data.

Segmenting data to analyse trends

Web analytics packages enable users to organise data in many ways, including location, demographic and channel. Segments let you separate and analyse subsets of data so you can examine and respond to the trends in your business. For example, you can investigate the underlying reason if you find that sales have dropped from users from a particular location. Maybe shipping rates are incorrectly configured?

Improving website performance

Once you have your website analytics package installed, you can start understanding your website's performance and looking for ways to improve it.

A webpage consists of several disparate elements, all of which influence your users. As a result, the only way to truly test page effectiveness is to change a page and see what happens. This involves:

1. **Analysis.** Scrutinise your analytics data to look for underperforming areas.

2. **Hypothesis.** Generate a testable hypothesis about your website. For example, if I make the buy now button green, it will increase revenue by 10%.

3. **Test.** Run an A/B test or a multivariate test, which are defined below, to test your theory.

Google Optimize

Google Optimize[58] is a free service that allows website owners to test changes in their pages' website content so owners can determine what affects conversions. You choose what parts of a page you would like to test, e.g. headline, image or promo text. Then you run an experiment on a segment of your site traffic so you can decide which content your site users respond to best. Two testing options are A/B and Multivariate tests.

A/B testing

A/B testing is when you present two (or more) versions of a web page to different website visitors to find which converts best. To do this, you specify the original page and alternative page arrangements you want to test. Google Optimize will split the traffic between the different versions, enabling you to establish the highest performing.

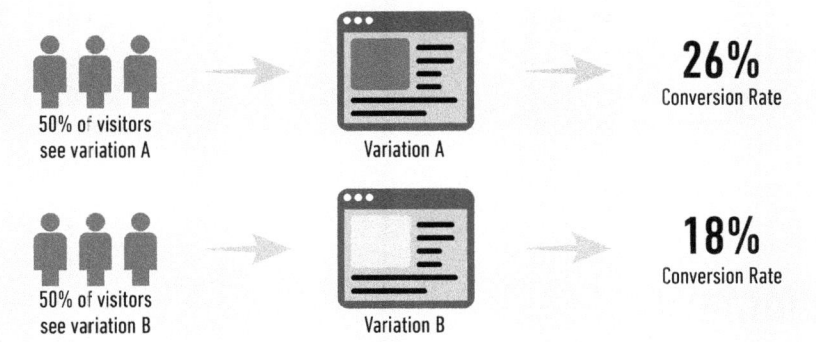

50% of visitors
see variation A

Variation A

26%
Conversion Rate

50% of visitors
see variation B

Variation B

18%
Conversion Rate

Fig. 6. A/B Testing

---

58 https://marketingplatform.google.com/intl/en_uk/about/optimize

A/B experiments are the simpler version of testing with Google Optimize. If you have low traffic and want results fast, creating an A/B test may be the right place to start.

Multivariate testing

Multivariate testing allows the testing of multiple variables simultaneously. For example, using multivariate testing, you could select the headline, image and promotional text on a page as your page sections and generate three different versions of each one. When the experiment was running on your page, a user might see Headline A, Image B and Promotional Text C together or Headline B, Image C and Promotional Text A.

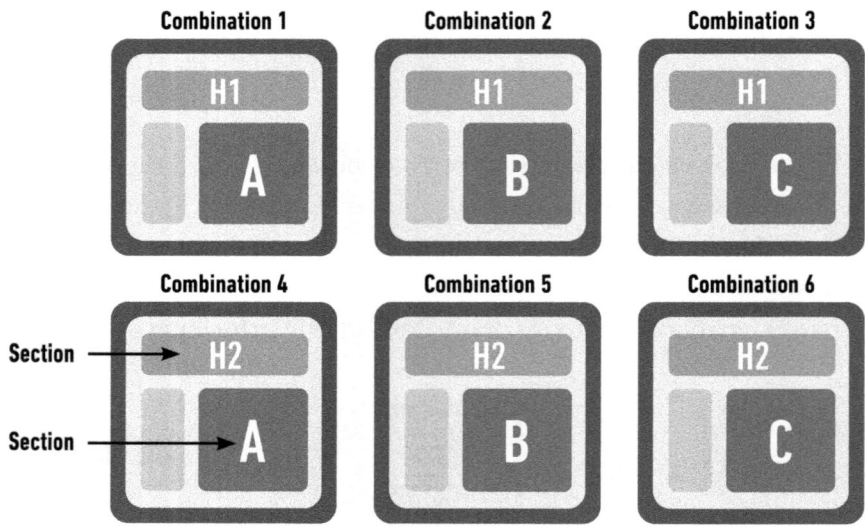

Fig. 7. Multivariate testing

Summary

Web Analytics will help your business understand your website's performance, your promotional activities' effectiveness and your customers' demographics. It will provide you with detailed information on what users are doing when they get to your site. You should decide on the key performance metrics for your business and monitor these closely.

With this information, you can make informed changes to the website's content and usability without spending more on advertising and improve your performance. Free tools like Google Analytics provide a rich array of reports or you can build your own by segmenting your data.

Resources

How well is your site doing? This question is difficult to answer as the answer varies by sector. Here are some valuable sources of information:

Conversion rate: https://www.smartinsights.com/ecommerce/ecommerce-analytics/ecommerce-conversion-rates/

Sales trends: https://www.irpcommerce.com/en/gb/ecommercemarketdata.aspx

Overall industry benchmarks: https://www.storegrowers.com/ecommerce-metrics-benchmarks/

4:

SEARCH ENGINE OPTIMISATION (SEO)

Google is a ubiquitous tool of the modern world, with 5.6 billion searches performed every day[59]. People depend on Google to answer all kinds of questions, including what products to buy. Google will serve up a list of results and ads for every query. About 75% of searchers don't make it past the first page[60]. Because of this, getting results for relevant queries onto the first page is vital to many businesses. Search Engine Optimisation refers to the practice of driving traffic from the unpaid (a.k.a. natural or organic) Google results. Paid search (covered in the next chapter) refers to performing well in Google ads.

I've been fascinated by search engines since I launched my first website. I became obsessed with optimising my site and building links. For a while, traffic was excellent and I thought I was a bit of a search engine genius. Then the Google Penguin update halved my traffic overnight. This was a sobering lesson for me as I depended too much on a single marketing channel.

Performing well in the search results for relevant searches is vital to businesses of all types who are looking to promote their products

---

59   https://www.internetlivestats.com/google-search-statistics
60   https://www.imforza.com/blog/8-seo-stats-that-are-hard-to-ignore

online. Unfortunately, due to poorly optimised websites, many companies underperform. Improving natural search traffic is a long-term project and it is easy to give up too quickly. However, it is worth persevering as SEO is one of the most cost-effective online marketing techniques.

Why Search Engine Optimisation (SEO)?

Thirty-five per cent of online product purchases start with a Google search (eMarketer[61]) and the volume of searches is growing by 10% per year (Source: Internet live stats[62]). This represents a huge opportunity to drive traffic to your website, increase sales and acquire customers.

Search Engine Marketing is the discipline of promoting your products or services through major search engines. Google has over 90% of the search market. Microsoft's search engine Bing[63] is a distant second with <5%). Search Engine Marketing has two sub-disciplines:

1. **Search Engine Optimisation (SEO).** Driving traffic by obtaining high placement in the non-paid (also known as organic or natural) search engine results.
2. **Paid Search.** Running targeted advertising campaigns on Google and, to a much lesser extent, Bing.

Creating an optimised search engine marketing campaign is demanding work. It requires an in-depth analysis of your market to uncover the search terms used to find products like yours (known as keywords) and constant monitoring and improvements to your site's

---

61   https://www.emarketer.com/content/more-product-searches-start-on-amazon

62   https://www.internetlivestats.com/google-search-statistics

63   https://www.bing.com

content so traffic is maintained. Fortunately, if your company lacks the resources for an all-out push, getting the basics right can make a marked difference to your online traffic.

The Search Engine market

Google has become the search engine of choice for most people globally and has 92% of the market (source: Statcounter[64]). Google has become so identified with Search that the phrase 'to Google' has become synonymous with 'to Search'.

While Google reigns supreme in the West, in China, the dominant player is Baidu[65] and in Russia, Yandex[66] is a significant player alongside Google. Bing is the number two website internationally, with less than 5% of the search market.

Search Engine marketing opportunities

The opportunities for businesses to promote themselves via search engines are Search Engine Optimisation (SEO) and Paid Search.

Search Engine Optimisation

Search Engine Optimisation is the process of configuring a website so it appears higher in the natural (free) search engine results for searches relevant to your business. These are the results on the left side of the Google results page generated by Google's search algorithm. Google takes no payment for positioning in these results and rank is based purely on Google's assessment of a page's relevance to a query.

---

64   https://gs.statcounter.com/search-engine-market-share
65   https://www.baidu.com
66   https://yandex.com

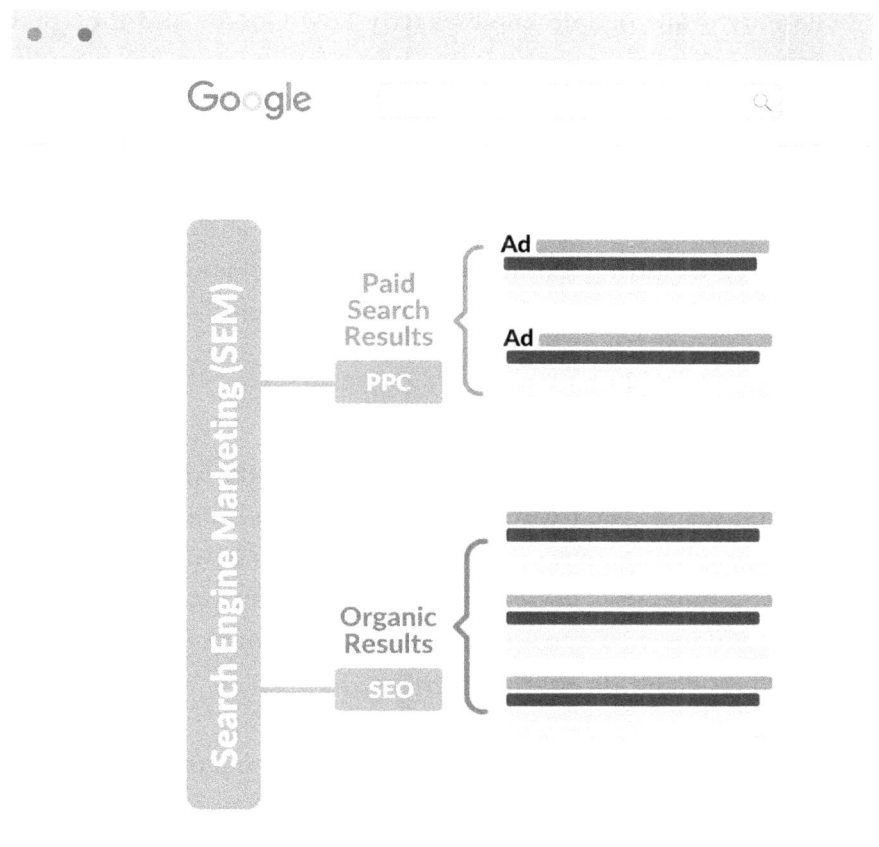

Fig. 8. Search Engine Marketing

To get significant traffic a website will need to appear at or near the top of the first page of the search results. Obtaining a high search result for a business is hugely valuable, as it can dramatically increase website traffic and, therefore, sales and brand awareness.

Google does not publish its algorithm and techniques for improving website performance are a matter of much speculation. This lack of clarity has led many charlatans to sell unsuspecting businesses expensive, ineffective solutions for improving rankings.

While only a few people know exactly how Google and the other engines produce their results, the influencing factors are broadly accepted. These techniques can dramatically affect traffic (see the section on ranking factors below).

As increasing natural search engine ranking is a lengthy and uncertain process, Search Engine Optimisation is often overlooked in favour of Paid Search. However, overall, it has the potential to be one of the most cost-effective sales channels for your business.

Paid Search

Paid Search refers to the adverts which appear on the top, bottom and right-hand side of the natural search results. Paid Search programs, such as Google Ads, have the potential to provide highly targeted, measurable and cost-effective traffic to your website. Typically, the adverts are charged on a pay-per-click basis, meaning that the advertiser only pays for traffic driven to their site.

To place an ad, an advertiser specifies a list of targets (traditionally keywords but these days also products and webpages) for which they want the advert to appear, the advert's text and the price they are happy to pay for a click. Google displays a list of adverts, triggered by the user's search term, next to the natural search results when a user searches. The adverts' order depends on the cost per click that each advertiser is willing to pay and each advert's past performance.

Unlike Search Engine Optimisation, Paid Search campaigns can be set up quickly and generate sales and traffic within hours. Furthermore, there will be enough data to tweak the adverts to improve performance after a few days. We will consider Paid Search in detail in the next chapter.

SEO Vs Paid Search

Research has shown that users tend to click on the natural search results about two-thirds of the time. Yet, despite this, companies spend two-thirds of their search engine marketing budget on Paid Search (Source: Moz[67]). This is for three reasons:

- **Speed of results.** Paid search campaigns can generate traffic quickly, while natural search campaigns can take months to show results.
- **Transparency.** Natural search traffic is at the grace of the search engine's algorithms. The system is transparent with a direct relationship between spending and traffic with Paid Search.
- **Tracking.** With Paid Search, it is easier to calculate the return on investment of the advertising spend. This is because it is possible to track sales from the moment someone clicks on an advert through to checkout completion. This allows return on investment and cost per conversion to be calculated accurately.

That said, I would encourage companies not to forgo investing in Search Engine Optimisation in favour of Paid Search. In the long term, SEO can provide an excellent return on investment. Overall, approximately two-thirds of search engine traffic to eCommerce sites comes from organic search[68], so it is a massively important traffic source. Furthermore, SEO is cost-effective because the search engines do not charge for inclusion in their listings. Costs associated with natural search are due to the initial and ongoing optimisation costs. However, investment in SEO should be a gift that keeps on giving as performance will improve over time. Furthermore, these are fixed costs, while Paid Search is a variable cost.

The following table summarises the differences between paid and natural search.

---

67   https://moz.com/blog/the-disconnect-in-ppc-vs-seo-spending

68   https://www.wolfgangdigital.com/kpi-2019

	Natural Search	Paid Search
Cost	Fixed: Cost of optimisation. No charge for listing.	Variable: Charged per click
Timescale for results	Months	Immediate
Control of traffic volume	Unpredictable – depends on search engine algorithm.	Dependable – traffic volume depends on budget.
Technical requirements	Yes – Require changes to website and site architecture.	None – No changes to the site needed.
Flexibility	Inflexible – Any changes made to a page will take several days for the search engines to register.	Flexible – changes to a campaign appear at once.
Return on investment	Difficult to measure.	Easy to measure.

Search Engine Optimisation and Paid Search can also be helpful for different things. SEO is good for gaining traffic from high-volume generic keywords/terms that generate a large traffic volume, e.g. 'convertible car'. These key phrases tend to be unsuitable for Paid Search as, due to their general nature, they have a high cost per click and do not often convert into sales.

Paid Search can be effective for targeting many low-volume keywords. Popular searches like 'car', known as the search head, get a significant traffic proportion. However, the sum of the less frequent but more specific searches such as 'BMW 3 series convertible' make up a similar or greater volume. This is known as the 'long tail'.

Key phrases in the long tail are likely to have a lower cost per click and have a higher conversion rate, as they are more specific. (compare 'car' with '2006 MW 3 series').

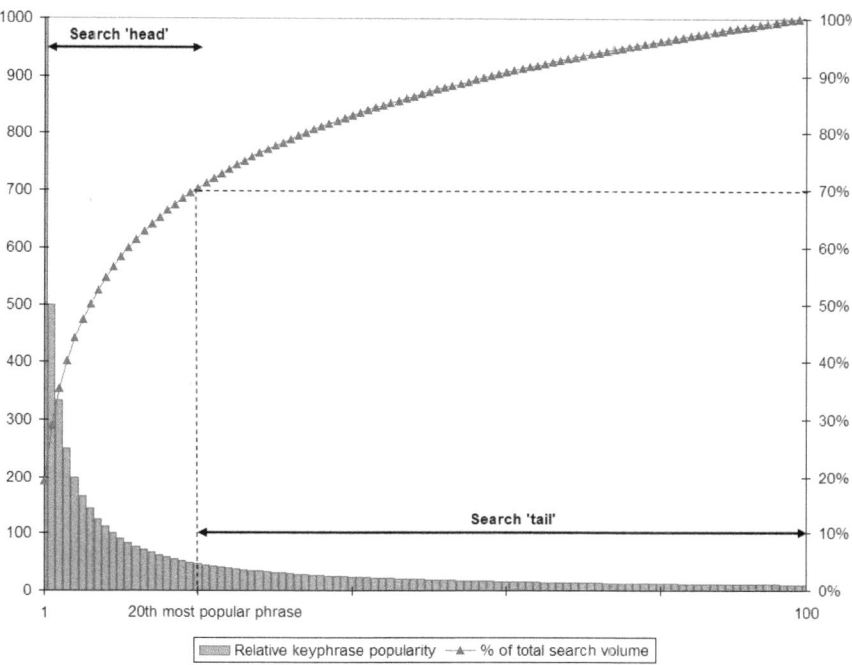

Fig. 9. The long tail

Optimising a website for all the key phrases that customers might use when looking for your products or services is impractical. However, with Paid Search, there is no (practical) limit on the number of keywords that can be targeted. Using Paid Search to target the search tail can be an economical way of driving targeted traffic to your site.

Tip: A site's search engine traffic should have a healthy balance between a Natural Search and Paid Search.

Search Engine Optimisation (SEO)

Having discussed the different types of Search Engine Marketing, the rest of this chapter will explain the techniques involved in Search Engine Optimisation. The next chapter will discuss Paid Search.

Why SEO is important

SEO is a vital part of any effective online marketing strategy. Organic search results are more trusted by consumers and receive more clicks than ads. Quality content that ranks well for important keywords will be a gift that keeps on giving, while advertising needs ongoing funding to send traffic to your site.

In summary, the benefits of SEO are:

- **Primary source of traffic.** The Google natural search results are the largest source of traffic in every sector (source: Growth Badger[69])
- **Cost-effective.** If managed effectively, SEO is a cost-effective method of traffic generation. The traffic is 'free', although there may be costs involved in generating traffic and getting the right advice.
- **Targets researching consumers.** SEO gets your business before your target audience, just as they actively search for information. This is because Google Search is the preferred first port of call for 62% of consumers (source: HubSpot[70]).
- **Branding.** Visibility on searches related to your business can positively impact your brand.
- **Sustainability.** Unlike Paid Search, organic traffic does not cease the moment you stop paying.

---

69   https://growthbadger.com/traffic-study
70   https://blog.hubspot.com/sales/buyers-speak-out-how-sales-needs-to-evolve

The Search Engine Results Page (SERPs)

Search Engine Results Pages (SERPs) are web pages displayed to users when they search online using a search engine such as Google. The user enters their search query and the search engine then presents them with a Search Engine Results Page (SERP).

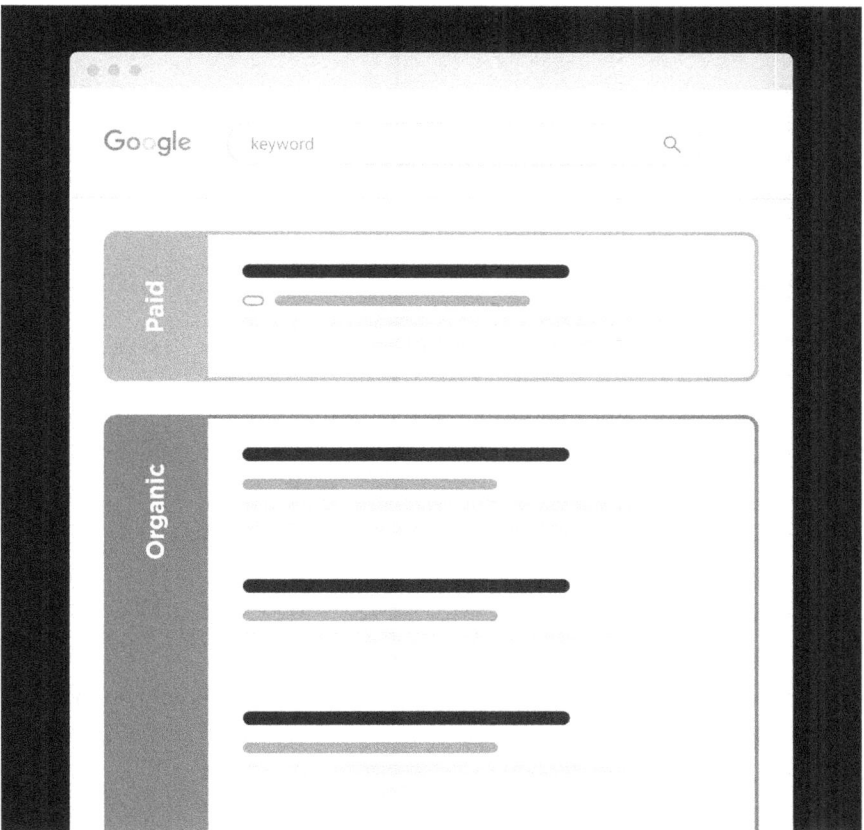

Fig. 10. Paid and Organic Search

Before optimising your website, you should understand how it might be displayed in the search results. Understanding the layout of a search results page can help you create content that encourages users to click your link. The SERPs now have dozens of features, but the most critical distinction is between 'paid' and 'organic' results and paid results.

The natural (or organic) search results are the listings of web pages generated by the search engine's algorithm. As discussed in the next chapter, the paid results are from advertisers bidding on keywords on Google Ads.

In the following figure, the results on the left are all organic (free):

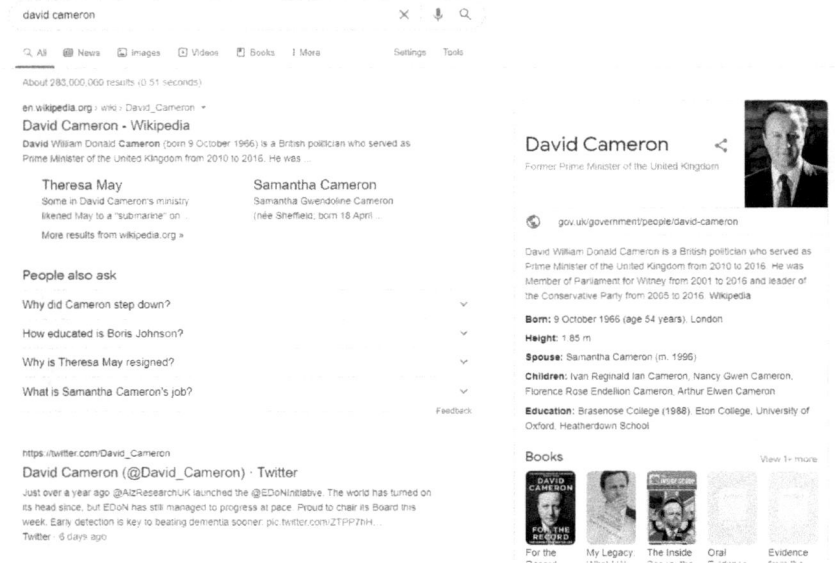

Fig. 11. The knowledge graph

On the right is the 'knowledge graph' (more details below). A standard organic search result includes:

- Page title. This is taken from the page's 'Title Tag'.
- Page URL. The 'Universal Resource Locator' i.e. the page's web address.
- Snippet. A summary of the page, taken from the page's content.
- Sitelinks. Some results will show further links to popular pages on the site.

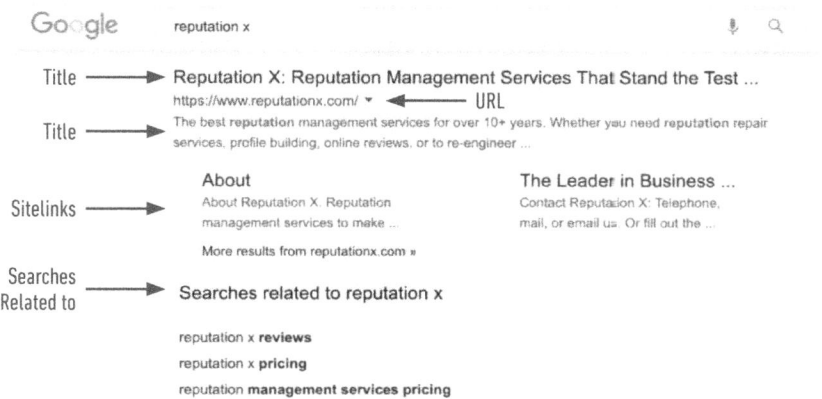

Fig. 12. Standard organic results

Title

This is the title tag for the page, which is defined in the page's HTML between the <title></title> tags. The title is the first and often only part of your search result that is read. Therefore, each page on your site should have an individual, descriptive title tag containing enough information to give the user a good grasp of the gist of the page.

Optimisation of title tags is covered in the content optimisation section below.

Sitelinks

Sitelinks are links that sometimes appear in the results below a listing's URL and meta description. Each Sitelink links to a leaf page within the current website and has a title and description. Sitelinks are more likely to appear in searches that suggest clear brand intent (e.g. searches for domains or brand names).

You cannot directly control the appearance of Sitelinks. Google's algorithm decides whether there are relevant Sitelinks on a website and whether to show them.

URL

Your URLs should be relevant and short but still give information about the page's content.

Snippet

The Snippet is the page's description and is limited to 156 characters. Google customises the snippet to each search query, using text from the meta description or page content.

Rich Snippets

Rich Snippets provide extra information to answer a query, such as a photo or a star rating. Adding structured data to your site can increase your chances of having a rich snippet displayed alongside your search results. A rich snippet looks like this:

Ultimate vanilla ice cream | BBC Good Food
https://www.bbcgoodfood.com/recipes/1881/ultimate-vanilla-ice-cream ▾
★ ★ ★ ★ ☆ Rating: 4,6 - 36 votes - 2 hrs - 269 cal
Ingredients. 284ml carton double cream. 300ml full fat milk. Milk. mill-k. One of the most widely used ingredients, milk is often referred to as a complete food. While cow... 115g golden caster sugar. 1 vanilla pod. 3 large free-range egg yolks. have lots of ice cubes at the ready.

Fig 13. Rich recipe snippet

This snippet contains a picture of the ice cream, a list of ingredients and other details.

Search Engine Results Page (SERP) Features

A SERP feature is any result on a Google Search Engine Results Page that is not a traditional organic result. SERP features can be paid or natural. Common features include:

Google Ads (paid)

These are paid ads typically purchased from Google on a pay-per-click (PPC) basis. Paid Search is covered in detail in the next chapter.

Knowledge panel (natural)

These are information panels that provide information about the main topic of the query. They appear near the top of the mobile results and on the desktop's right-hand side (see the figure above on David Cameron, the former British Prime Minister).

Featured snippets (natural)

These show a content snippet from a top-ranking web page. They appear at the top of the search results.

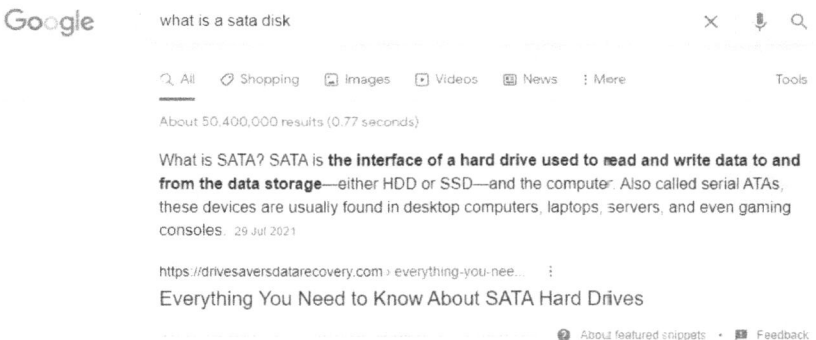

Fig. 14. Featured snippet

Knowledge card (natural)

This appears at the top of the results and offers a short answer to a query. The example below is a knowledge card showing Google's response to "What is the weather today".

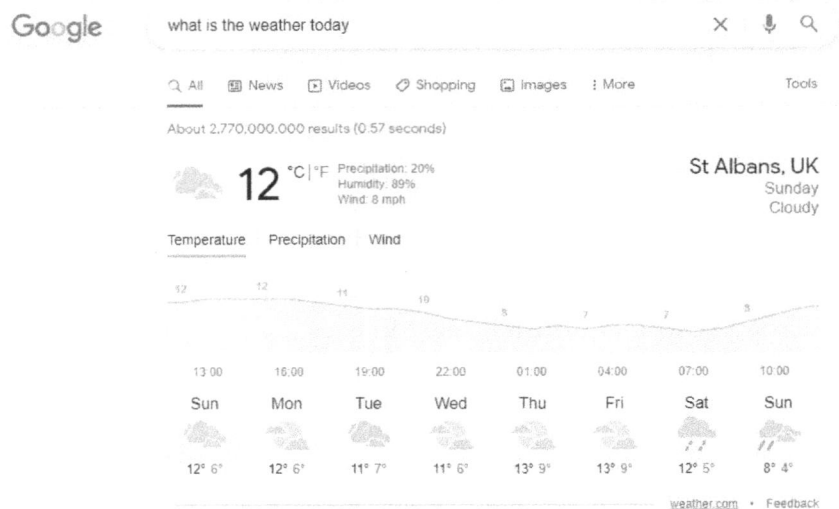

Fig. 15. Knowledge card

Image pack (natural)

Image Packs show several thumbnails. Clicking on them takes you to Google Images.

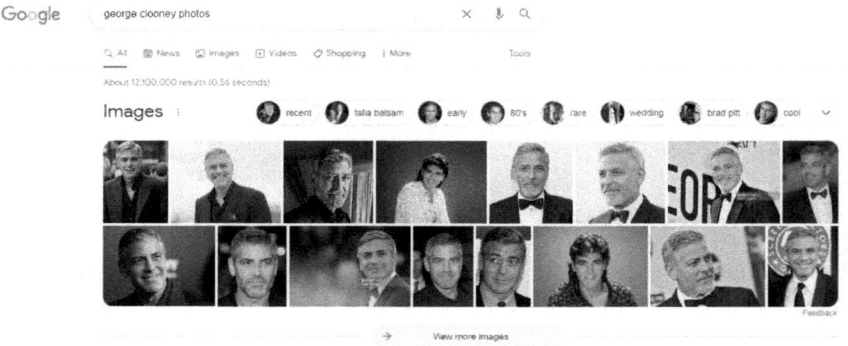

Fig. 16. Images Rich Snippet

Top stories (natural)

The Top stories carousel shows recently published articles, live blogs and videos.

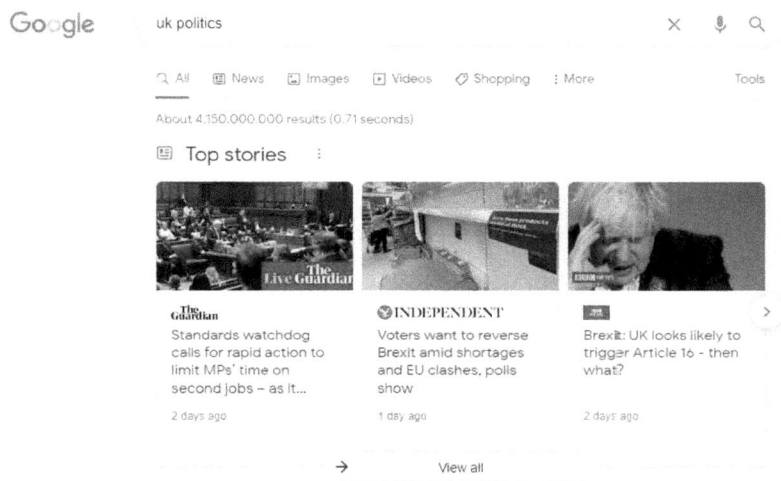

Fig. 17. Top Stories rich snippet

Google Maps

Google Maps provides local information for places around the world. Google Maps data often appears in search results, especially for local queries. It includes aerial maps, road maps and Street View maps taken from Google vehicles.

Adding your business to Google My Business[71] is free and especially important for companies with local customers such as physical shops. By creating a Google My Business profile, your business information will appear in relevant local searches, generating free traffic for your business.

Tip: Google is changing all the time. Read sites such as Moz and Search Engine Land to stay on top of developments.

---

71   https://www.google.com/business

How Search Engines work

Search Engines perform a marvellous feat. Based on a text query, they produce a list of (usually) relevant results from the billions of pages on the World Wide Web. Moreover, they do this at lightning speed, with search results appearing as you type.

Crawling and Indexing

Search Engines do not achieve this by searching the web but by accessing a massive web content database called the Search Engine's 'Index'. This database holds information about the content of millions of websites (e.g. text, images, videos) and their links. The Search Engines use automated programs called Robots (a.k.a. spiders, bots or crawlers) to investigate new websites and record any changes to pages already in their Index. This process is known as Crawling. New content will be discovered by following links.

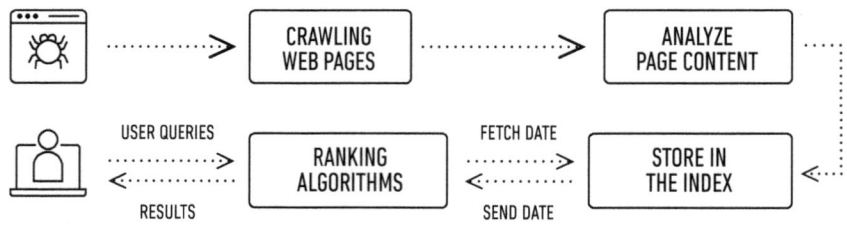

Fig. 18. Indexing and crawling

Ranking

When someone performs a search, search engines will interrogate their index for the most relevant content for that query and present that to the user. The ordering of results by relevance is referred to as Ranking. A search engine's method of indexing the web and producing a list of results for a given query is referred to as its 'algorithm' and is a closely guarded secret. Algorithms are complex and look at multiple factors when deciding on the ranking for each query. Industry experts believe that Google uses over 200 ranking factors[72] when compiling results. Ranking factors include:

Quality and Quantity of Links

Using link relationships was Google's incredible insight and enabled it to build a much better search engine than the competition. Instead of just looking at a site's content, Google considered links to that site from other sites. A link to a site was treated as a vote of confidence, with content with more incoming links ranking higher.

Links are not created equal and links from more established sites will improve ranking more. All other things being equal, the more natural backlinks you have from trusted, high-authority websites, the better your chances of ranking higher within search results.

Content relevancy

Your page's rank for a query is decided by how well your page's content matches Google's perception of the searcher's intent. The process of 'On-page Optimisation' involves researching the best keywords to target your site's pages and creating content that utilises these keywords (process discussed below).

Performance metrics

Google is constantly revising its search results by considering performance data. It uses performance metrics such as click-through rate and time on site and machine learning techniques to tweak its search results in real-time. This produces more relevant results.

For example, if a lower result gets more clicks than a higher result, it will be judged to be more relevant. Google may then move that result up the list to respond to user behaviour.

---

72   https://backlinko.com/google-ranking-factors

Fig.19. How search results change over time

Improving Natural Search performance

Goals and Key Performance Indicators (KPIs)

Before you start working on the Search Engine Optimisation of your website, think about what you are trying to achieve and how you will measure it. This will establish the site areas you should focus on, track conversions and let you know if you are successful.

Set Key Performance Indicators (KPIs) for your SEO campaign (and your online marketing in general). These might be:

- Sales
- Downloads
- Email signups
- Contact-form submissions
- Phone calls

These high-level business goals do not include details like ranking and traffic. Therefore, the traffic you drive from your SEO activities is only helpful if it helps you achieve your business goals.

Black Hat or White Hat Search Engine Optimisation (SEO)

Search engine optimisation techniques divide into Black Hat and White Hat SEO.

Black Hat SEO

Black Hat SEO techniques try to trick search engines into thinking that a website is relevant for a particular search term. They do this by manipulating weaknesses in the search engine's algorithm. One example of an old black hat technique is using white text on a white background to increase a particular term's occurrence. Black Hat techniques depend on reverse-engineering the search engine algorithm and are sensitive to algorithm changes.

White Hat SEO

White Hat SEO techniques build long-term traffic through quality content and relevant links from other highly ranked sites. The aim is to create a site optimised for search engines that provides a pleasant experience for users.

While all of Search Engine Optimisation is an attempt at reverse engineering, White Hat SEO is not about 'chasing the algorithm'. Instead, it is about building a website's prominence while staying within the guidelines set by Google and the other major search engines.

White Hat or Black Hat?

Black Hat techniques can generate traffic in the short term. However, they are hypersensitive to changes in the search algorithm. Furthermore, using techniques not approved by Google puts websites at tremendous risk of being penalised or de-indexed (removed from search results). This can be disastrous if your business depends on natural search traffic for a sizable proportion of your sales.

White Hat techniques play by the rules to create a site that will receive traffic over a long period, building an asset for its owners. Google has published a list of excellent guidelines for optimising websites[73] and, if you do what they say, you cannot go wrong! Their recommendations include:

- Make pages firstly for users, not for search engines.
- Do not deceive your users.
- Avoid tactics intended to boost search engine rankings. A helpful test is to ask, does this help my users? Would I still do this if search engines did not exist?
- Consider what makes your website special. Make your website distinct from others in your field.

Tip: Google can and does penalise sites breaking its rules. Don't risk it.

Elements of Search Engine Optimisation (SEO)

As discussed above, producing search engine results involves several distinct processes and many factors must be considered when building and maintaining a high-performing website.

- **Crawling.** The ability of search engines to find your pages and read their contents.
- **On-page SEO.** Creating compelling content which answers and informs searchers' queries and ranks highly for relevant key phrases.
- **Technical SEO.** Building your site in a way that maximises natural search performance.
- **Off-page SEO.** Building your site's authority by link building and online Public Relations (PR).

---

73   https://developers.google.com/search/docs/advanced/guidelines/overview

Crawling: can Search Engines find your pages?

Before your website can appear in the search engine results, it must appear in the search engine's index. Therefore, the first task of optimising your site must be to determine whether any issues prevent your site from being fully indexed. Unfortunately, many sites are constructed in a way that prevents search engines from indexing some or all the pages on the site.

Analysing current performance

Establishing what proportion of your site's pages is indexed is essential. Do this by comparing the number of pages on your website (as measured by your content management system) with the number in the search engine's index. To find the number of pages from your website that Google has indexed, consult the Google Search Console (see below). Then, to estimate the proportion of indexed pages, divide the number of indexed pages by the total number of pages.

It takes time for a search engine to refresh its index. Therefore, if your site is large or often changes, 100% inclusion is unlikely. However, investigate if the number of pages indexed is way below the expected level (see below). If your site is not appearing at all, then there could be a few reasons for this:

- New site that has not yet been crawled.
- No links from external websites.
- Site navigation makes it difficult for a robot to crawl it.
- 'Crawler directives' are blocking search engines. e.g. robots. txt file
- Site has been penalised by Google for 'Black Hat' tactics.

Google Search Console and Google Sitemaps

Google has created a suite of tools called Google Search Console[74] (GSC) with the mission of helping you measure your site's search

---

74   https://search.google.com/search-console/about

traffic and performance, fix issues and also make your site shine in Google Search results.

The tools supplied include:

- **Coverage reports.** See the number of pages that Google is indexing.
- **Search performance.** Natural search clicks and performance as measured by Google.
- **Website analysis.** Google's analysis of the quality of your website, e.g. usability and page speed.
- **Google sitemaps.** A sitemap is an XML (Extensible Markup Language) file that, when submitted to Google, provides details of the pages on your site. Submitting a Google sitemap is crucial to improving your indexing and should be a priority after a site launch. These will be generated automatically from all decent Content Management Systems (CMS) and eCommerce systems and quickly submitted to GSC.

Indexing problems

If your site is not being indexed or has a low percentage of indexed pages, one of the following problems may be present:

Robots.txt file

There are some excellent reasons why you would not want a search engine to index sections of your site, for example, admin, checkout pages and duplicate content.

Robots.txt files can be found in the root directory of each website (e.g. vendlab.com/robots.txt). They tell Google which parts of your site it should not crawl. A problem with the robots.txt file may cause Google to stop crawling your site.

Inaccessible content

Your content could be inaccessible to search engine crawlers for several reasons:

- **Search required.** If the content is only accessible via a search, it will not be accessible to the crawler.
- **Non-text content.** Do not use non-text media formats (e.g. images and video) to display text you wish to have indexed.
- **Non-HTML menus.** Search engines have difficulty reading menus not written using HTML, e.g. JavaScript.
- **Navigation dead ends.** Crawlers only find pages linked to other pages.

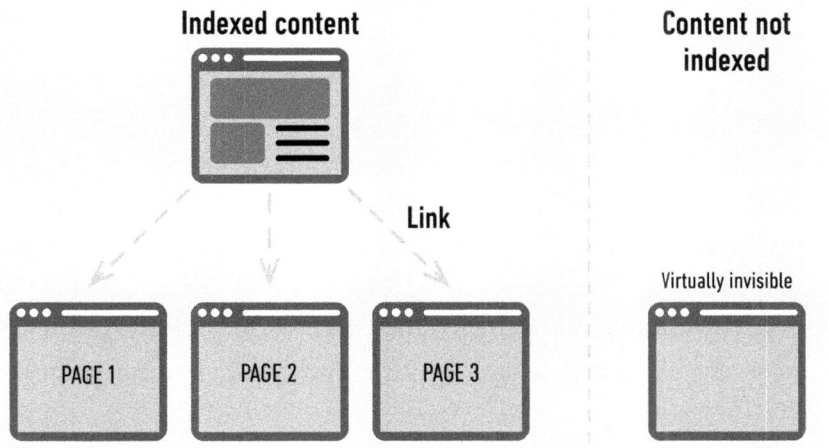

Fig. 20. Inaccessible content

Server Errors

When crawling the pages on your site, a crawler may encounter errors. Google Search Console's 'Crawl Errors' report lists URLs where there are server errors and 'not found' errors. A moved page will lose its ranking unless the site sets a '301 redirect' to direct the page visitor to the new location. A redirect will ensure that the new page is indexed correctly and maintain its authority.

On-Page SEO

On-page SEO optimises individual web pages to rank in the search results and drive more relevant traffic. On-page SEO includes both the content and HTML source code of a page.

It has the following components:

- **Keyword research.** Deciding the target keywords for your site's content.
- **Content creation.** Creation of readable, high-quality content that also attracts search engine traffic. Examples include how-to articles, blogs that are frequently updated and FAQs.
- **Technical SEO.** Configuration of a website to ensure that it is search engine friendly.

Keyword research

Because of the enormous range of search phrases entered by users, a vital task of on-page SEO is to decide the search terms for which to optimise your company's website. The choice of keywords is based on an analysis of your company's business. The aim is to generate a list of target keywords and analyse search demand. From this list, you select the most appropriate keywords for which you wish your site to rank.

Once the keywords have been researched, organised and prioritised, amend the site's content to include these keywords. New content can be created if a relevant page does not exist. In the past, pages were optimised for individual keywords, with website owners aiming for a target 'keyword density'. However, Google's search algorithm has become more sophisticated so it is best to identify target keyword groupings around which to build a topical page.

The search journey

When selecting keywords, it is necessary to put yourself into the user's mind and imagine how they find a product or service. Searchers use various kinds of key phrases at the different buying cycle stages. Searchers go through three steps (the search journey) when investigating products.

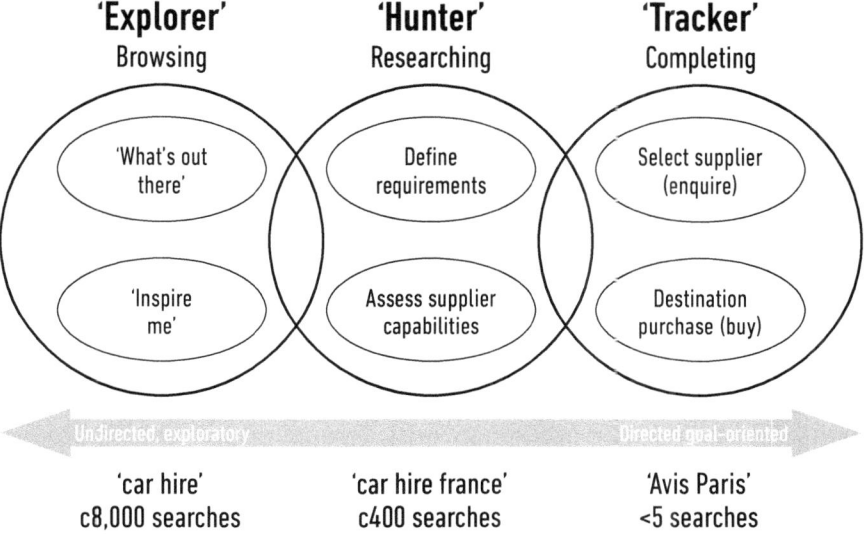

Fig. 21. The search journey

- **Browse.** Broad search terms are used to investigate a product area, e.g. *car hire*. Due to their general nature, these are high volume searches but do not convert well.
- **Research.** More specific searches intended to home in on the right product. e.g. *car hire France*
- **Buy.** Search terms used when people are looking to purchase, e.g. *Avis Paris*. These phrases convert well but are low volume due to their specific nature.

Your site should provide content aimed at each of the different sections of the search journey. Furthermore, it is essential to understand the part of the search journey at which your pages are aimed and select your keywords accordingly.

Generating a search term list

The following sources can be used to generate keywords:

- **Google Search Console search query report.** This lists the natural search queries that drove traffic to the site.
- **Google Keyword Planner[75] tool.** This keyword discovery tool provides search volumes for key phrases on the Google platform.
- **Competitor websites.** Analyse competitor's sites to establish the key phrases for which they have optimised their sites.
- **Paid search data.** If you run a paid search campaign, data from this can inform your keyword choice.

Once you enter your seed keywords into a keyword research tool, you will begin to discover other keywords, frequent questions and topics for your content. Once generated, organise keywords into groups according to the themes.

Analysing and selecting search terms

Once you have generated your list of themed keywords, analyse and organise them to establish where the opportunities lie. Using a spreadsheet, place the keywords in one column and complete the following columns:

- **Search volume.** Obtained from Google Keyword planner.
- **Search competition.** Obtained from Google Keyword planner
- **Current performance.** Your current ranking for the keyword. Tools such as Ahrefs[76] offer a free trial. Also, include your traffic data from Google analytics.
- **Intent.** Where in the search journey does the keyword lie?
- **Theme.** Grouping similar keywords together to establish themes.

---

75   https://ads.google.com/intl/en_uk/home/tools/keyword-planner
76   https://ahrefs.com/keyword-rank-checker

Deciding keywords to target

Typically, higher search volume means greater competition and more effort to achieve organic ranking success. On the other hand, low-competition keywords may not drive much traffic. Therefore, it may be most helpful to target a range of specific, lower-competition search terms in the search 'long tail'. There are a small number of high-volume keywords, but most searches are across many lower-volume keywords. This effect is known as the 'long tail'.

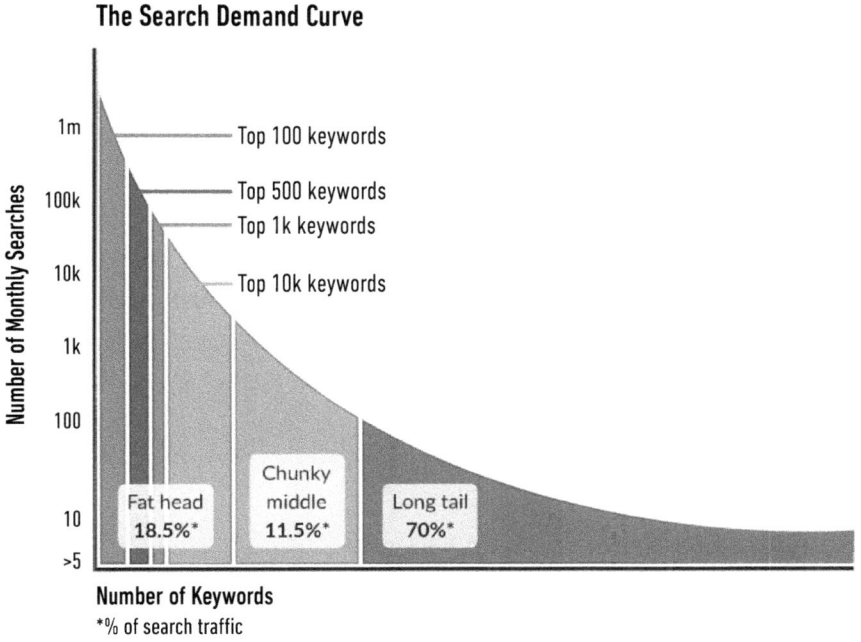

Fig. 22. The search demand curve

While long-tail keywords are lower in volume, they may be more specific and convert better. For example, the keyword '30-inch curved monitor' is more precise than 'monitor'.

By looking at the keywords you have found, you will discover keyword popularity, competition and current performance. From this, you will be able to see:

- **Underperforming areas.** Consider creating content based on these themes, e.g. blog posts, how-to guides or other resources.
- **Areas in which your site is currently ranking on page 2 are 'low-hanging fruit'.** Improving this content may be enough to push the result onto page 1 and massively improve traffic.
- **Well-performing keywords.** Monitor these keywords to ensure that they stay on top.

In each of the themes targeted, choose a primary keyword and several secondary keywords to incorporate into the text. The content should be readable and not just for search engines.

Content optimisation

The next stage is to integrate target keywords into your site to increase your chances of achieving favourable positioning in the Search Engines Results Pages (or SERPS). The goal is to create pages judged to be highly relevant to your business' target search terms (as established in your keyword analysis).

Avoid thin content

Google states that you should have a comprehensive page on a topic instead of multiple, weaker pages for each keyword variation. Concentrate on creating fewer pages of higher quality. For product category pages, merge categories with few products to ensure that all categories have a decent number of products.

Avoid duplicate content

Google ranks original content higher, and your site should aim to generate as much high-quality, original content as possible. Duplicate content is shared between sites or between multiple pages on the same site. Examples include manufacturers' descriptions used without editing.

Google does not penalise duplicate content as such. It does, however, filter identical versions of content from their search results. Some duplicate content is unavoidable (e.g. if you have a site for different geographical regions). Use the *rel=canonical* tag to point to the original version of the content.

Body text

The main content on the page is the body text or copy. Avoid 'keyword stuffing' and focus on naturally writing content, including variations and related keywords to show topical authority. Include the primary keyword in the page's first paragraph, ideally in the first 100 words.

Keyword stuffing is the practice of inserting many keywords into content to artificially increase a page's ranking in search results and drive more traffic to the site.

Header tags

Header tags are HTML tags that define page headings and sub-headings. Every page should have one H1 tag describing the page's primary topic. As the page's main descriptive title, the H1 tag should contain that page's primary keywords.

<h1>Page Title</h1>

Sub-header tags go from H2 to H6 in descending order of importance. Headings introduce content to improve readability.

Internal linking and anchor text

A website's crawlability depends on its internal linking structure. Linking to other pages on your site ensures that crawlers can find all your site's pages, passes link equity (ranking power) to other pages on your site and assists users in navigating your site.

Another linking factor to consider is the anchor text which is the text with which you link to pages. The anchor text signals the content of the destination page to search engines. For example, if you link to a page using the text 'Car Seat Guide', Google may take this as a sign as to the content of the destination page. Be careful when doing this, as too many links to a page with identical anchor text may make Google think you are trying to game the system. It is best to link to a page using a range of different anchor texts.

Images and video

Videos and Images are a great way to increase engagement, reduce bounce rate (the percentage of visitors who view only one page) and increase dwell time. In addition, alt text (alternative text) tags for images are vital for web accessibility as they describe images for visually impaired browsing. Search engines also crawl image alt text to understand your photos, increasing your ranking for key phrases in text and image search.

Title tags

A page's title tag is an HTML element that specifies the page's title. It is placed within the head tag of each page like this:

<head> <title>Example Title</title></head>

Placing target keywords in the title can help users and search engines understand your page's content. For example, if your keywords are close to the beginning of the title tag, then users are more likely to read them and hopefully click on the content. Keep it short, as Google will trim title tags longer than 70 characters.

Meta Description

The meta description is an HTML element that outlines the contents of a page. They are also positioned in the head tag and look like this:

<head> <meta name='description' content='Description of page here.'/></head>

The meta description field will influence the text on the search result page (see above). The attributes that make an effective title tag also create compelling meta descriptions. While Google says that meta descriptions are not a ranking factor, they are important for click-through rate.

Search Engine friendly URLs

If a page's URL contains the keywords for that page, the search engines may rank the pages more highly for those keywords. This works for two reasons. Firstly, using the keywords in the URL will reinforce the page's relevance to that search term. Secondly, the text will automatically include the target keywords where the page is linked by name.

This approach can work at the domain name level, e.g. www.arenaflowers.com contains the keyword for its main product, i.e. flowers and for pages lower down in the page hierarchy such as products, e.g. http://www.arenaflowers.com/flowers/occasion/birthday_flowers. Besides natural search performance, search engine-friendly URLs help users understand the page's content.

Technical SEO

Google aims to serve its users with high-quality sites which quickly answer their queries. Consequently, it has started to consider various factors related to the site's performance and technical architecture. Since the technical structure can have a massive impact on its performance, it is essential to understand the factors affecting performance.

JavaScript

Most websites use JavaScript to add interactivity and improve the user experience. For example, it is frequently used in menus to pull in products or prices. However, the dynamic nature of JavaScript has historically caused issues with search engine crawling. If Google cannot access the menus on a site, it may have difficulties reading the content.

Google has stated that if you are not blocking the Googlebot from crawling your JavaScript files, they can read JavaScript as a browser can. However, it can take Google longer to index JavaScript content. Therefore, it is best to check that Google can read your pages correctly. This can be done from within Google Search Console using their URL Inspection Tool.

Schema

Schema is a way to label or organise your content so that search engines can better understand your web pages. Schema provides structure to your data which is why it is often referred to as 'structured data'. The process of structuring data is often referred to as 'markup' because you are marking up your content with organisational code.

JSON-LD is Google and Bing's preferred schema markup. Visit Schema.org to view a complete list of the thousands of available schema markups. Besides helping bots like Google understand what a particular piece of content is about, schema markup can also enable rich snippets (mentioned above) to accompany your pages in the SERPs.

Page load speed and usability

As well as being vital factors in your site's conversion rate, page speed and website usability are also ranking factors considered by Google. These factors are combined into Google's *Core Web Vitals* measures available in the Google Search Console.

To benchmark your site's performance, use Google's PageSpeed Insights[77] tool and measure your page speed and identify improvement opportunities.

---

77   https://developers.google.com/speed/pagespeed/insights

Mobile friendliness

In 2020, mobile internet usage exceeded desktop usage for the first time. In response to this, as of March 2021, Google will stop indexing desktop versions of a website and only index mobile-friendly sites. Therefore, making your website compatible with mobile screens is necessary for maintaining search performance. It also creates a better experience for most users who access sites via mobile devices. To ensure a good mobile experience, Website owners should implement the following:

- **Responsive design.** Responsive websites adjust to the size of the user's screen.
- **AMP.** Accelerated Mobile Pages (AMP) deliver content to mobile visitors faster.

Off-page SEO: building website authority

Google's great insight that allowed them to build a better search engine was the value of links as a mechanism for differentiating between sites. Whereas earlier search engines just looked at the text on a page, Google considered the relationships between sites. Each link was considered a vote and sites with many incoming links (often referred to as backlinks) were given higher search rankings.

Whilst Google has changed a lot since its early days, links are still among the most important ranking factors for SEO. In the past, getting a lot of low-quality links or buying links would work as a strategy. However, it is essential only to get high-quality links relevant to your business these days. Conversely, avoid inferior quality links as they will not help a site rank better and harm your natural search performance.

Best practices for link building are as follows:

- Build relevant, quality links.
- Create great content to which people want to link.

- Aim for a range of links from various sources with different anchor text.
- Do not buy links.
- Avoid low-quality sites.

Link building strategies

Building links is more complex than it used to be and many tactics that worked well in the past, e.g. directory submission or blog comments, no longer carry any weight. So, focus on building links organically from high-quality sources (see leading link building service FAT JOE[78] for a list of quality link sources).

Create high-quality content

Quality content provides more content for the search engines to index and provides 'link bait'. Sites with excellent content will naturally receive links from other sites whose owners believe the linked content is valuable for their visitors. Quality content can take the form of text, applications and resources such as how-to guides.

Links from partners

Other websites will be happy to link to high-quality sites which share similar or complementary content. With links, aim for quality over quantity as it is better to get fewer, higher-quality links.

Sources of links can include:

- **Business partners.** Ask your business partners to recommend your services by placing a link to you on their site.
- **Suppliers.** Many suppliers will have a list of resellers on their sites.
- **Quality directories.** There are often specific local business directories that promote nearby businesses.

---

78   https://fatjoe.com/link-building

Websites that link to your competitors are an excellent source of links. There is a free backlink check on Neil Patel's site.[79]

Online Public Relations (PR)

Generating stories about your business is an excellent way of getting quality links to your site. One way to create media interest is to submit press releases to relevant media websites. Media websites tend to be well indexed. Search engines rank them highly as they contain a large volume of quality content that attracts links and are often updated.

Target the following types of media sites when distributing new stories:

- **Blogs.** Many bloggers are hugely influential in their fields and may be interested in writing about your product and services.
- **Press release sites.** Websites that accept and distribute press releases. Some of these sites are free and others charge a small fee.
- **Online magazines.** Online magazines and newspapers often write stories after direct approaches and press releases.

Ongoing optimisation

Search Engine Optimisation of a website is not a one-off job. You should constantly measure performance and tweak your website to get the best results. Google and the other major search engines often change their algorithm. This means that if your site is top of the ranking today, it may not even be on the second page tomorrow.

To ensure that your website stays well-ranked and attracts significant traffic from the major search engines, keep the site's content fresh by

---

79   https://neilpatel.com/backlinks

constantly adding new content and ensuring that it receives a constant trickle from quality incoming links. As with all forms of online marketing, measuring your performance using a good web analytics package is vital.

Summary

Search Engine Optimisation is the process of building traffic from Google's free (a.k.a. natural or organic) search results. Search Engine Optimisation is one of the biggest opportunities available to eCommerce businesses. It drives approximately two-thirds of search engine traffic to websites and is the largest single traffic source for many companies.

Optimising a website involves structuring it to be read easily by search engines. The next step is to create high-quality content, optimised to include customers' search terms to search for your products. Finally, building links to the website from quality websites grows a website's authority and boosts search rankings.

Unlike Paid Search, driving traffic from Google natural search is a long process and the results are not guaranteed. Competition for high rankings is fierce and 75% of clicks go to page one listings. However, optimising your site can provide a cost-effective way of generating traffic and increasing sales. In the long run, money spent on SEO should give a good return on investment.

Resources

Some excellent industry websites have a wealth of up-to-date information on SEO, including on- and off-page SEO and technical SEO.

Moz – https://moz.com

Search Engine Land – https://searchengineland.com

Ahrefs – https://ahrefs.com

Google also has a guide to SEO called Google central (https://developers.google.com/search). An excellent place to start!

5:

SEARCH ENGINE MARKETING: PAID SEARCH

Whatever is thought about Google, it is hard to see its search engine as anything less than a miraculous tool that makes our lives better. I use it hundreds of times a day and it usually generates relevant results. However, every time I have tried a competitor, the experience has been disappointing and I have beaten a hasty retreat.

Of course, as the saying goes, "if you do not pay for a product, then you are the product". The ads which appear alongside the natural search results are the money machine that turned Google into one of the biggest companies in the world.

For many retailing businesses (including my own), advertising on Google is a significant sales driver. My retailing company generates about half its website sales from Google Ads. They are easy to set up, monitor and optimise and can start generating business pretty much immediately. After marketplaces, they should be the next strategy you should explore to grow your business.

What is Paid Search?

Paid Search Marketing refers to the adverts which appear next to the natural search results in search engines like Google and Bing. Typically, the adverts are charged on a pay-per-click basis, meaning that the advertiser only pays when a user clicks on an advert and goes to the advertiser's site, not just when the advert shows.

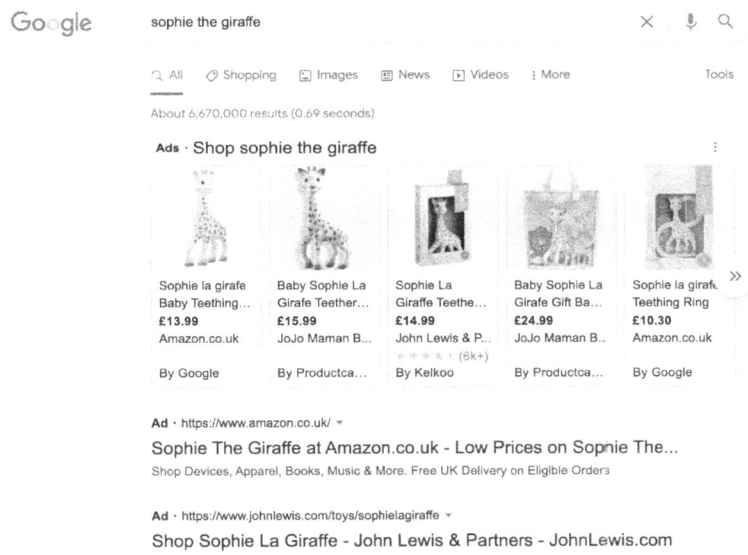

Fig. 23. Paid Search ads

Paid Search programs, such as Google Ads, have the potential to provide highly targeted, measurable and cost-effective traffic to your website. For queries relevant to your business, advertising alongside the search results targets potential customers researching or buying a product. Whilst Google Ads are primarily about driving website traffic, they can also increase in-store visits or phone calls.

Microsoft's Bing search engine also has an advertising program. However, in this chapter, we will focus on the Google Ads program, which has the lion's share of the market.

Here are some key stats:

- Advertisers make £8 in revenue for every £1 they spend on Google Ads (Source: Google[80]).
- Google Ads have a click-through rate of 8%.
- Google Ads convert 50% better than organic search results (Source: Wordlead[81]).
- 65% of Ads clicked contain buyer intent keywords, e.g. buy, shop, purchase, get, cheap, for sale (Source: Wordlead[82]).

Paid Search fundamentals

When users search on Google, it will generate natural and Paid Search results. Both results are ranked with the most prestigious position at the top. If a user clicks on a Paid Search result, they are taken to the advertiser's website and the advertiser is charged. The advertiser is only charged when an advert is clicked, so this system is known as Pay-Per-Click (PPC).

Fig. 24. Paid search process

---

80   https://static.googleusercontent.com/media/economicimpact.google.com/en/static/reports/2016/ei-report-2016.pdf

81   https://www.wordlead.com/facts/ppc-statistics-adwords-trends/

82   Ibid.

Benefits of Paid Search

Google Ads enable advertisers of all sizes to reach customers worldwide when they are searching for products and services. Before Paid Search, national advertising was out of the reach of most small businesses. However, Paid Search has levelled the playing field, allowing small businesses to advertise on the same platform as larger businesses.

Benefits include:

Cost

There is no minimum spend on Paid Search networks and you only pay when users click on your ads.

Fast and easy to use

Unlike Search Engine Optimisation, a simple Paid Search campaign can be set up in a few minutes and generate traffic and sales within hours.

Self-service

Google Ads is a self-service platform that is simple to use. Employing external agencies to manage campaigns is not necessary for most businesses.

Flexible

Adverts can be changed at any time to focus your message and optimise performance.

Worldwide reach

Google has a worldwide reach and advertisers can create adverts that target multiple locations and languages from the same account.

Targeted

Paid Search adverts are contextual to each search, targeting users researching products. Advertisers can also target by (amongst other things) location, device, demographics and time of day.

Range of formats and wide distribution

Google Ads has a diverse range of ad formats to suit every business type, including search ads, shopping ads and retargeting. Alongside Google search, they can also serve your ad across the broader Internet via their wider network, which includes:

- **Search network.** This includes the Google search results page, Google properties, e.g. Google Maps and Google Shopping and partner search sites that show text ads.
- **Display network.** Focuses on platforms and advertising methods that are not text-based. Display network sites include platforms like YouTube, Gmail and thousands of partner sites.

Unavoidable

As seen in the example above, Paid Search often takes up most of the page 'above the fold' (i.e. the screen's content without scrolling). Thus, as the natural search results are pushed down the page, Paid Search is sometimes the only way to get noticed.

How Paid Search works

To place an advert, advertisers specify a list of keywords (or sometimes landing pages or products) for which they want the advert to appear, plus the advert's content and the price they are willing to pay for a click. Google displays a list of adverts next to the natural search results. These are triggered by keywords in the search query when a user searches. The adverts' order is decided by the cost per click the advertiser is willing to pay and by the advert's historical performance.

For example, imagine an online retailer wants to advertise its range of digital cameras. They create an advert triggered by the key phrase

'Canon digital camera'. A user then uses Google to search for 'buy Canon digital camera'. The advert may be served if the search phrase contains the specified keywords. If a user clicks on the advert, the retailer is charged. If not, there will be no cost.

Calculation of Cost-Per-Click

Google uses an auction-style bidding process to set prices when deciding what to charge advertisers. For any two adverts of the same quality score (see below), Google will award the higher position to the ad with the highest bid. However, the winning bidder will pay only slightly more than the loser.

For example, suppose there are three ad slots available and four advertisers competing for those positions. The table below shows each advertiser's maximum bid and, if their ad is clicked, the amount they end up paying:

Advertiser	Position	Max Bid	Amount Paid
Ad 1	1	£4	£3.01
Ad 2	2	£3	£2.01
Ad 3	3	£2	£1.01
Ad 4	4	£1	Ad not shown.

How Ads are Ranked

Google displays Paid Search results in order, just like organic search results. The position of an ad has a significant impact on traffic. To decide the relative positioning of ads, Google has devised a score called *Ad Rank*. The higher an ad scores, the better its position.

Ad rank is decided by:

- **Bid amount.** All other things being equal, bidding higher means higher rankings.
- **Quality score.** A measure of the relevancy of the ad to the query.
- **Context of search.** Google will look at the searcher's details (e.g. location, device and time) in relation to your ads.

Ad Rank recalculates each time an ad is eligible to appear and competes in an auction. Therefore, its position fluctuates depending on your competition, search context, and quality score.

Quality Score

The Quality Score is Google's measure of the quality of a search query/advert combination, i.e. how relevant the advert is to the search query.

Quality score is decided by:

- **Historical Click-Through Rate.** CTR indicates how relevant the advert is to its associated keywords.
- **Ad relevance.** Google will analyse whether the ad is relevant to the search query.
- **Relevance of the landing page.** Google analyses the landing page's content to judge the page's relevance to the advert and keyword. For example, imagine you are bidding on a competitor's brand name and the advert directs users to your website where your competitor's brand name is not mentioned. In this situation, Google will analyse the landing page and may increase its minimum bid for this keyword.

The quality score rewards relevant, high-performing ads with a higher position at a lower cost per click. For an advert to get an elevated position, it is not enough to bid high; you also need to have a superior quality score.

The diagram below shows how the entire process works:

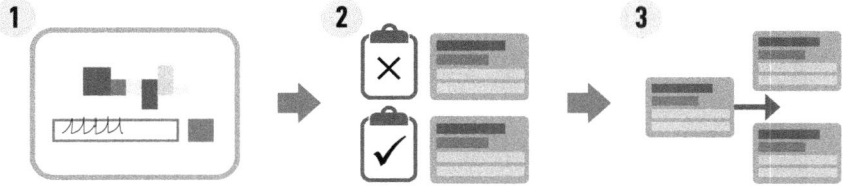

Fig. 25. How Google selects ads to display

1. Google identifies all the ads with keywords matching that search when someone searches.
2. From within those ads, Google ignores any that are ineligible, e.g. those that target a different location.
3. Of the remaining ads, only those with a sufficiently high Ad Rank may display.

Ad distribution

Google Ads do not just appear on Google's search pages (i.e. Google. com). Advertisers also have the choice to allow their ads to appear on other sites within Google's Display Network and Search partners.

Google Display Network

The Google Display Network consists of over 2 million websites. When you choose this option, your campaign will run on the Display Network with no additional setup. As a result, your ads will appear only when predicted to be effective and you are not using all your budget on search.

Search Partners

Google search partners are search sites that show Google Ads on their search results.

Example sites include:

- **Amazon.** Ads are displayed alongside search results.
- **Guardian.** This site uses Google custom search[83] to power site search.
- **YouTube.** YouTube is the world's second-largest search engine.

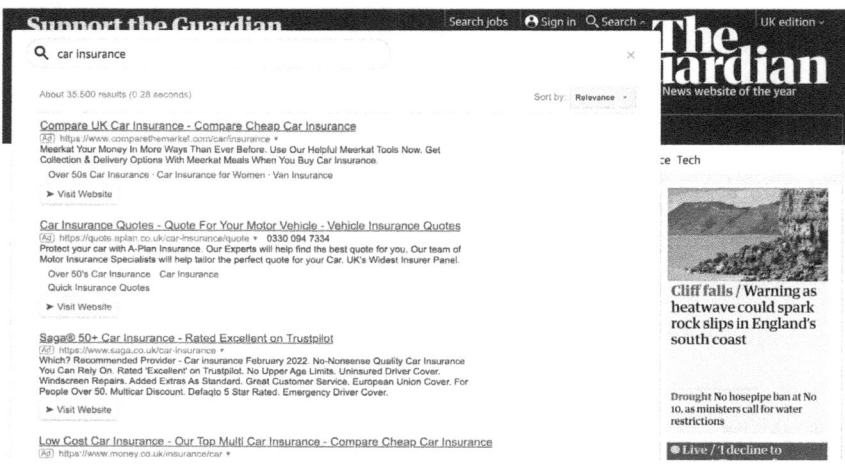

Fig. 26. Search Partner Network site

Should you advertise on Google's partner sites?

The benefit of Google partner sites is that they enable your ads to reach a much wider audience. Search results pages make up a tiny fraction (around 5%) of all pages viewed online and the Google Network lets advertisers reach a wider internet audience. Google analyses each page's content and examines the text, language, link structure and page structure. It then serves the most relevant ads.

Advertisers can opt-in or out of partner sites and Google provides performance reporting that separates out Google Network sites. You can always include the partner sites initially and exclude them if they do not meet your performance targets.

---

83   https://programmablesearchengine.google.com/about

Budgets and bidding

Budgets

Budgets on Google Ads are set at a daily level, averaged over a month, i.e. some days you may be under your daily budget and some days above, but you will not overspend over a month. The Shared Budget option allows you to distribute one budget across multiple campaigns, with Google automatically adjusting the budget allocation.

Tip: Start your campaign on a low budget so you do not spend money too quickly while getting up to speed.

Ad delivery method

There are two options for pacing how often Google shows your ads:

- **Standard.** The campaign budget is spread evenly throughout the day (or when your ads are scheduled to display). Your ads will show throughout the day but they may not always display as, to ensure the budget lasts the entire day, Google holds back delivery.
- **Accelerated.** Delivery is not optimised to help your budget last through the day. Instead, it aims to ensure ads will show as often as the auction allows. Depending on the budget, the ads may not display all day.

Bidding options

When running Google campaigns, you have the option of managing bids manually or using Google's automatic bidding tools. With Google's automated bidding, you are charged on a CPC basis. Google will automatically alter bids based on its estimation of the likelihood of a conversion to meet a specified goal.

Whilst some advertisers still prefer the control they get from managing campaigns manually, automated bidding is a time-saver. Furthermore, automated bidding is based on machine learning and will improve over time. Automated bidding strategies include:

- **Target CPA** (Cost per Acquisition). You set your target CPA (how much you are willing to spend per conversion) and Google will try to place bids to meet that CPA target.
- **Target ROAS** (Return on Advertising Spend). This strategy aims to maximise revenue or conversion value. This is based on the target return you set on ad spend.
- **Maximise Conversions.** This strategy tries to get the most conversions within your daily budget.
- **Enhanced CPC (ECPC).** This strategy raises the max CPC in auctions that the algorithm predicts are more likely to convert and lowers the bid in auctions considered less likely to convert.

Tip: Using Google's automatic bidding is a massive time-saver. In my experience, it is just as good as 3rd party software solutions and it is free!

Measuring campaign performance

There is little point in running any advertising campaign if you do not track its effectiveness and act on this information. One of Paid Search advertising's great benefits is that it is highly trackable. As a result, return on investment can be calculated in a way that is just not possible with most traditional forms of advertising.

Tracking

Conversion tracking helps you understand how effective your campaigns are at getting users to take the actions you want, e.g. sign up for your email or make a purchase after they click your search ads.

To enable sales data to be passed back to Google, you will also need some code on your site's page and link your Google Analytics and Google Ads accounts.

When setting up conversion tracking, there are several selections to make:

- **Conversion type.** If you are an online retailer, the chances are you are most interested in sales. Other conversion types include an email sign up and white-paper downloads.
- **Conversion window.** The conversion window is the maximum time you want to count a conversion after someone clicks your ad. Remember that some users will purchase several days after viewing a product.
- **Attribution model.** Customers may visit the same site via several different paths — in which case, how much of the sale is attributable to Paid Search? One option is to attribute all the sales to the last website visited, though this may underestimate the contribution from Google Ads. For example, a customer may find a website using Google Ads and then use a cashback site to get a discount. Using last-click attribution will mean that all the sales are attributed to the cashback site. This is the simplest option but does not fully capture the Google Ads contribution to the sale.

Once tracking is implemented and the accounts linked, conversion data will be available directly in your Google Ads account. See Chapter 6 for more information about Web Analytics.

Tip: Understanding your performance is critical to optimising your campaigns. Take time to get your tracking correctly implemented.

Important metrics

There are four basic metrics for PPC ad campaigns:

- **Impression.** An impression is the number of viewers to whom the ad is displayed. Impressions measure how often Google has displayed your ads, i.e. how relevant it considers your ads are to its users.
- **Click.** A click is an instance of a viewer clicking on an ad. This measures the amount of traffic (i.e. the attractiveness) of your ad to users.
- **Conversion.** A conversion is when a viewer views an ad, clicks it and takes the action you intend them to take on your landing page. Conversions are a measure of the success of a campaign, as a conversion will typically be a sale.
- **Spend.** Spend is the amount of money you have spent on your campaign within a specified period. Your target ratio of spending to revenue will depend on your business objectives. For example, is it is more important to keep spending low or to get more sales at a lower margin?

These metrics are essential to track but, for optimising your campaigns, the measures that will be the most critical derive from combinations of these simple metrics.

These measures are:

Click-through Rate (CTR)

Click-through Rate is the percentage of ads that are clicked. A high click-through rate indicates that your advert is attractive to users. Google uses the CTR as an input in its quality score so a high CTR will positively affect your cost per click.

CTR (Click-through Rate) = Clicks / Impressions

Conversion Rate

Conversion Rate is the percentage of clicks that lead to a conversion. A higher conversion rate will reduce your *Cost-Per-Click* and *Cost-Per-Acquisition*.

Conversion Rate = Conversions / Clicks

Cost-Per-Click (CPC)

Cost-Per-Click (or CPC) is the amount of money spent on each click. Average CPC is calculated by dividing the spend by the number of clicks. Therefore, a lower cost-per-click will reduce your Cost-Per-Conversion.

CPC = Spend / Clicks

Cost-Per-Acquisition

Cost-Per-Acquisition (or CPA) is the amount of money spent to get each conversion. The average CPA is calculated by dividing the total spend by the total number of conversions.

CPA (Cost-Per-Acquisition) = Spend / Conversions

An effective campaign has high-percentage metrics and low-cost metrics. It is good practice to set goals for your campaign performance in terms of these metrics. Watch these metrics closely as you continue optimising your keywords, ads, and account structure. Use them to measure your campaign's performance as you work toward reaching your goals.

Setting goals

When running any advertising campaign, set goals against which to measure performance.

Example goals include:

- **Number of clicks or impressions.** If you are trying to gain exposure for a new product, you may be interested in getting the maximum number of clicks or impressions out of your budget.
- **ACoS.** *Advertising Cost of Sales* is the % of the sale value spent on advertising. Depending on your margins, you could look to keep this below a certain level.
- **ROAS.** *Return on Advertising Spend* is like ACoS but looks at the ratio of sales to advertising spend.
- **Cost-Per-Acquisition.** If you are looking at a customer's lifetime value, you might set a target cost-per-acquisition.

Targeting

Google Ads enables advertisers to create highly targeted ads by adjusting for many aspects of user behaviour. For example, an advertiser can optimise campaigns by changing bids based on performance and excluding unprofitable segments.

Options include:

- **Networks.** Ads are always displayed on Google search, but the advertiser can also select Google search partners and Google display network.
- **Locations.** Select the geographical location where the ads will be served at the country level (UK, France or US) or target local areas down to individual postcodes. Advertisers can also make 'bid adjustments' on regions based on relative performance (e.g. +10% for London, -10% for Edinburgh).

- **Language.** Choose the language preference of your target customers. For example, you could choose to target French speakers in Switzerland.
- **Audience.** Audiences are groups of users that Google has labelled as having specific interests, intents and demographics, e.g. toys, childcare, shopaholics.
- **Devices.** Advertisers can specify bid adjustments based on the users' devices. For example, +10% for desktop, -10% for mobile.
- **Ad schedule.** advertiser can increase or decrease bidding for specific periods of the week or stop advertising entirely.
- **Demographics.** Adjust bids based on the demographics of users, e.g. income, age, gender.

Tip: By targeting your ads, you will increase performance and reduce spending. If you notice that a group of users is converting at a lower rate, they can have their bids reduced or excluded entirely. You should constantly monitor your performance from within the Google Ads interface and a Web Analytics tool such as Google Analytics (see Chapter 3)

Landing Pages

How well your ads convert traffic into sales will largely depend on the quality of the page you send them to – the landing page. Therefore, the design and overall structure of your page design will have a massive impact on the effectiveness of your landing page and how well it drives conversions. The primary goal of your landing page should be to make it very easy for a visitor to convert. Because of this, it is essential that all elements of your page work towards this objective, i.e. filling out a form, making a purchase or signing up for a newsletter.

Good landing pages will have the following features:

- **Relevant to the advert.** The content on the page should match the message of the advert or the user will leave immediately
- **Clear offer.** As soon as visitors land on the page, they know what the company offers. This includes the product information, price and delivery details.
- **Calls to action.** The calls to action should be prominent, e.g. the 'add to basket' button.
- **Visually attractive.** The page should make good use of imagery and be uncluttered.

Platforms such as Shopify have honed the design of their product pages to ensure a high conversion rate. If you are designing your landing pages, there are plenty of templates online that you can use as a basis for your design (see Resources at the end of this chapter).

Campaign structure

Structure a Paid Search campaign carefully, as a good structure allows for easier account management and more targeted campaigns. Google Ads campaigns are built in a hierarchical structure, as shown below.

Account

Each advertiser has an account where they specify their payment details and user access levels. To illustrate, let us imagine that the advertiser is a seller of computer equipment based in the UK:

Campaign

A Paid Search account contains one or more campaigns. Variables such as budget, language and location are set at the campaign level. Our retailer might select campaigns related to their primary product lines, desktops, laptops and monitors.

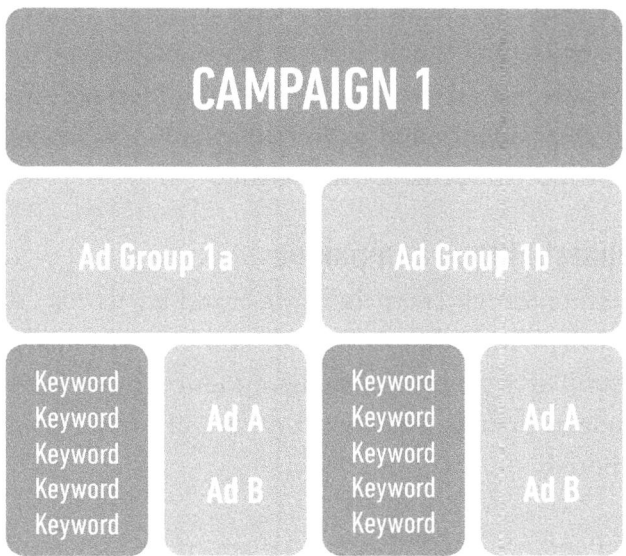

Fig. 27. Google Ads campaign structure

Ad groups

A campaign consists of one or more Ad Groups. Each search ad consists of a list of keywords and one or more adverts that they wish to appear when the keywords are searched. Bids are specified at the ad group or individual keyword level.

In our example campaign, the retailer has Ad groups Lenovo, Dell and Sony.

Organising campaigns

Keep Your Ad Groups targeted

Organise Ad groups into themes with keywords and ad copy on the common theme. Ads will be most successful if ad copy is relevant to the search. Conversions will be highest when searchers are taken to a page corresponding to the ad's content.

Break down your campaigns so that each ad group targets a specific product or service and the number of keywords is kept small. Using 15-20 keywords per ad group will keep the message targeted and improve ad performance and conversion rates. The more ad groups you have, the more targeted the messaging.

Create separate brand campaigns

Create separate Search campaigns for brand keywords. Your brand campaigns will perform differently from non-brand campaigns as these users are familiar with your business, products or services. You will want to budget, manage and report on brand campaigns separately from non-brand.

If the brand and non-brand campaigns are created separately, be sure to add brand keywords as negative keywords (i.e. customer searches for which you do not want your ads to appear) to your non-brand campaigns. Doing this will direct all brand traffic through your brand campaign.

Network-specific campaigns

Where a choice is available, do not target more than one network in each campaign. Google search and display networks can perform quite differently.

Keep it simple!

Whatever structure you opt for will need to be monitored and maintained. Creating a structure with separate ad groups for each product will theoretically improve targeting. However, in practice, it will be too hard to support.

Types of adverts

Google Ads have been around for 20 years and have evolved into a complex suite of ad types. These include:

- **Search.** Text ads which appear alongside the Google search results.
- **Display.** Text, image or rich media ads which appear on the Google search network.
- **Video.** Video ads that appear on YouTube and other video partners.
- **Shopping.** Carousel ads which display products alongside the Google search results.

Search

Search ads can appear at the top and bottom of results pages on desktop and mobile. A maximum of four text ads appears at the top of mobile and desktop search results.

Creating a search campaign has the following stages:

- **Campaign structure.** As discussed above, Google campaigns are organised into campaigns and ad groups.
- **Generate keywords.** Specify the keywords for which you wish your ads to appear.
- **Create adverts.** Create compelling adverts which encourage viewers to click through to your landing page. The landing page should be relevant to the ad and not just send users to your homepage.
- **Optimise.** To get the best performance out of your campaigns and improve performance, you need to constantly tweak your ads, targeting, bids, and landing pages.

Keywords
Keywords are the fundamental building block of every Google Search Ads campaign. Keywords trigger adverts that viewers click and are taken to your website. Therefore, finding relevant keywords is a core activity in creating and optimising a Paid Search campaign.

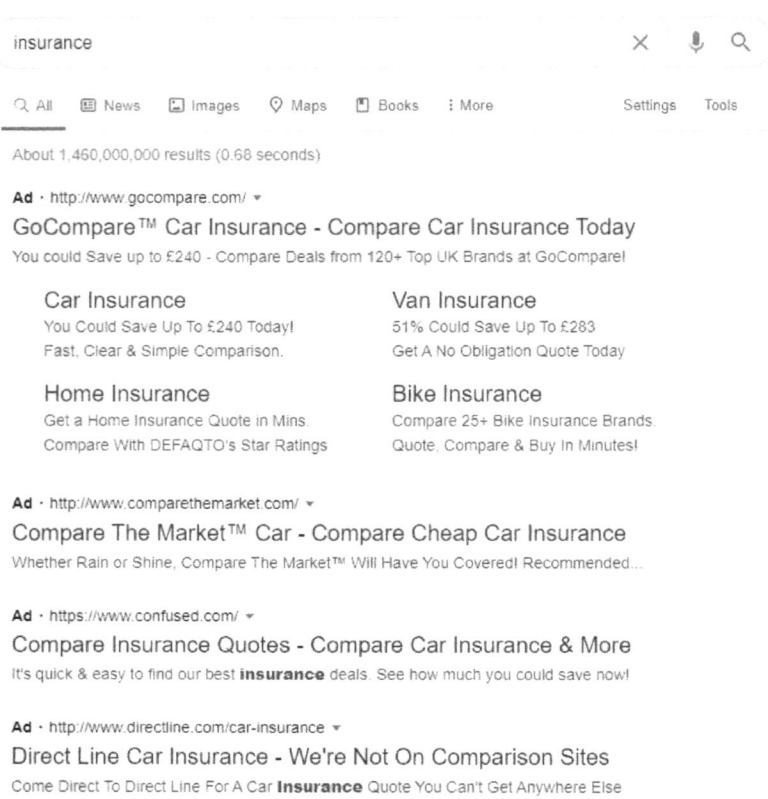

Fig. 28. Search ads

It does not cost to add keywords to a Google Ads campaign and having many 'long tail' keywords, whilst keeping the cost-per-click low, can generate quality traffic.

Keywords selection is a process of generating keywords by choosing the most relevant and then organising them into ad groups. Once the ads are created, constantly refine keyword choice based on performance.

Keyword generation

The first step is to generate as many keywords as possible and record your findings in a spreadsheet. Cast your net far and wide. To help in this effort, you can draw on the following resources:

- **Knowledge of the marketplace.** Think of the different searches people could use if they were looking for your products. Include product names, industry terms and commonly used alternatives. For example, adhesive tape can also be called Sellotape, sticky tape, duct tape or scotch tape.
- **Analytics data.** Look at the searches driving people to your website from the natural search results.
- **Competitors' websites.** Analyse competitors' websites to see the keywords which they are ranking. Tools such as Moz's Keyword Explorer[84] help with this.
- **Keyword generation tools.** Keyword generation tools such as the Google Keyword Planner can generate keywords based on keywords you have entered or your website's text.

Group

These keywords will be used to create campaigns and ad groups. Group your keywords into topics or product groups. Keep each group small, aiming for around 15-20 words.

For example, you might wish to organise your ad groups according to your products, e.g. Canon digital camera, Casio digital cameras.

Match types

By using keyword matching types, adverts will be seen only by the desired audience, reducing unwanted clicks, increasing conversions and decreasing costs. For example, if you are selling new items, you may want to stop your adverts from appearing for searches that include the words 'second hand' or 'used'. Adding these as negative keyword matches prevents your ads from appearing when these queries are used.

---

84 https://moz.com/explorer

There are four match types:

Broad Match

Broad Match is the most inclusive matching type and is the default option for all new keywords. A Broad-matched keyword will trigger ads even if there are other keywords in the query. The order is not important.

For example, for the broad match keyword 'Canon camera'

Canon digital camera	} Ad will appear
digital Canon camera	} Ad will appear
pink Canon digital camera	} Ad will appear
Canon printer	} Ad will not appear
Canon toner	} Ad will not appear

Phrase Match

A phrase-matched keyword will trigger an ad only when the query includes your keywords in the exact order specified.

For example, for the phrase-matched keyword 'used car':

used car dealer	} Ad will appear
buy used car	} Ad will appear
vintage used car	} Ad will appear
used sports car	} Ad will not appear
used sports car dealer	} Ad will not appear

Exact Match

'Exact match' only triggers an ad when the query contains the keyword exactly as typed in the keyword list.

For the exact match keyword ' used cars'

Used cars	} Ad will appear
Used car dealer	} Ad will not appear
Used car	} Ad will not appear

Negative Match

Negative matching prevents ads from appearing when a search includes a word that is not relevant to your ad. Negative matching enables advertisers to stop adverts from appearing for irrelevant searches, saving costs and increasing conversions.

For the negative keyword 'used':

BMW dealer Chelmsford	} Ads would appear
Find BMW dealer	} Ads would appear
Used BMW Dealer	} Ad would not appear

Use of Matching Types

Advertisers should use all matching types in their Google Ads campaigns. One strategy is to use each keyword in broad, phrase and exact match types. Google will then choose the most appropriate type for each query.

The use of negative keywords is a must for all Google Ads customers. To generate negative keywords, use data about the actual searches that drove traffic to your site and analyse them for unsuitable queries. This data can be obtained directly from Google Ads (the search query report) or your web analytics package.

Writing Ads

Google Search Ads consist of two headlines, a description, display URL paths, destination URL and ad extensions. Google suggests adding three or more ads to every ad group and at least two ad versions in each ad group. When more than one ad is specified, ads will be tested against each other, allowing you to tweak the ads to improve performance.

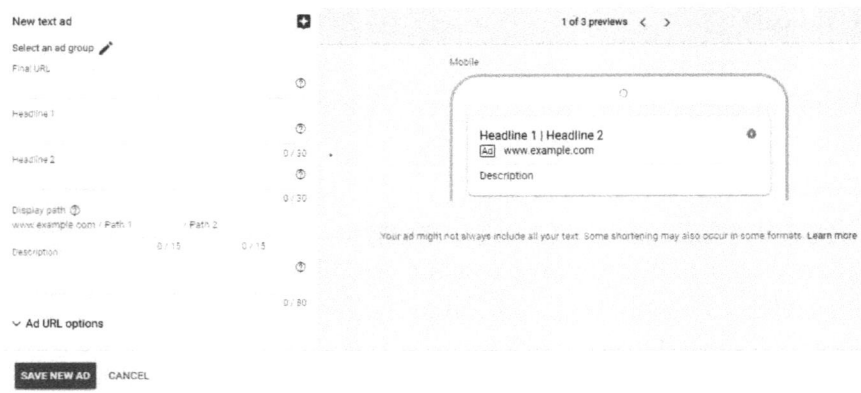

Fig. 29. Creating a Search Ad

Headline

Each headline can be a maximum of 30 characters, including spaces. Two headlines must be specified and they appear on one line at the top of the ad, separated by a pipe or dash. The headline is the most prominent part of the ad and should catch the searcher's attention. The headline can set itself apart from other ads by stating a benefit, feature, or offer.

Description

The description can have a maximum length of 80 characters, including spaces. You can experiment with the length and content but it should always reflect the search intent.

Display path

The display URL is set automatically to the domain from the final/ destination URL. You can then set two paths of 15 characters each that show after the URL. For example, an ad displayed for the search term 'mens jackets' might use one path of /jackets or two paths of / mens/jackets.

URL

This is the landing page to which users will be directed after clicking your ad. Be sure it is relevant to the search query and provides a good user experience.

Ad extensions

Ad extensions add additional information to your ad. There are many ad extensions and Google regularly introduces new types. Based on device and location contexts, ad extensions are automatically generated in combinations predicted to improve click-through rates.

In 2013, Google included ad extensions in its Ad Rank calculation, meaning that the extensions used influence the price you pay per click and your ad's position in the search results. Highly relevant extensions can result in lower CPCs and higher page placement. For this reason, advertisers are encouraged to add every applicable ad extension into their campaigns. Google generates some extensions, such as Sitelinks, automatically.

Ad · http://lp.boughtbymany.com/pet/insurance ▾
Get A Quote Today - Over 300,000 Pets Covered
Get A Quote With The Voted Best **Pet Insurance** Provider 2020 at the **Insurance** Choice Awards

Comprehensive Pet Cover	15% Off Multipet Discount
Up To £15,000 Vet Fees/Year	15% Discount For More Than 1 Pet
Pet Insurance Built To Pay Out	Claim This Discount On Our Website
Pre-Existing Conditions	Easy To Make A Claim
We Cover Past Medical Issues	No Forms Required - 97% Claims Paid
Find Out More On Our Website	Find Out More

Fig. 30. Example of an advert with a sitelinks extension.

Some examples of extensions:

- **Sitelink extensions.** These are clickable extensions that link to site pages. The number of sitelinks that can show with an ad is two to six on desktops and up to eight on mobile devices.

- **Callout extensions.** Callouts highlight offers and benefits to users. Examples of callouts include *Free Shipping, Free Returns* or *Shop Our New Arrivals*.
- **Price extensions.** These highlight service and product category offerings. Each price extension includes a customisable header and a description of up to 25 characters. Google suggests setting up at least five price extension items. You can set these up in bulk with a spreadsheet template.
- **Promotion extension.** Promotion extensions are clickable, appear with a price tag icon and include two text lines about the promotion.

Dynamic Search Ads (DSAs)

Creating and optimising multiple search ads is a lot of work. However, Google has introduced a product that will automatically create ads based on your site's content.

To set up a DSA campaign, the advertiser specifies a list of targets, e.g. landing pages or a product feed (a file containing a list of products in a specific format). Google crawls your site and then matches it to search terms closely related to your site's content. The advert's headline is also automatically generated to match the search term. This allows consistency between the search term, the search ad and the landing page.

DSA bidding

DSA campaigns charge on a cost-per-click (CPC) basis like search ads campaigns. However, unlike regular search campaigns, you do not apply bids to individual keywords since DSA does not use keywords. Instead, you will need to specify bids at the landing page level (targets).

Pros and cons of DSAs

DSA campaigns are hard to distinguish from regular text ads. They have the following advantages:

- **Increase keyword coverage.** DSAs allow advertisers to quickly close gaps in keyword coverage and the coverage of product inventory.
- **Easy ad creation** Writing ads is easy as the headlines are dynamically generated based on the page matched to the query. While you still need to write a description, the dynamic headline is most important as that will grab users' attention and drive more clicks to your site.
- **Easy to set up.** DSAs are easy to set up as no keywords are needed.

On the downside, as these ads are dynamically created, you surrender much control. Consequently, monitor new DSA campaigns to ensure they are performing.

Display

The Display Network uses Google's vast number of website partners to display your ad on different websites all over the Internet. Depending on the ad type, ads are charged based on cost-per-click, cost-per-action or cost-per-1000 impressions (referred to as CPM).

Types of Display Ads

Ads on the display network are available in several different formats:

- **Text ads.** Google search ads that advertisers select to publish on the display network.
- **Image ads.** These ads allow you to use images on the display network to get people to click through to your website.

- **Rich media ads.** Rich media ads are like image ads but have interactive elements, making them more compelling.
- **Video ads.** Like rich media ads but feature an embedded video.

Display Ad targeting

Advertisers bid on keywords to determine where ads display on the search network. However, the Display Network works differently, with advertisers choosing placement and targeting type:

- **Contextual targeting.** By selecting keywords, contextual targeting aims to get adverts onto websites relevant to the advertiser.
- **Placement targeting.** Placement targeting allows advertisers to choose the sites they wish their ads to appear.
- **Remarketing.** Remarketing is where you advertise to people who have already visited your website. Typically, these are display ads that promote specific products the users had previously viewed. The goal is to entice them back to the site.
- **Topic targeting.** Choose the websites advertised upon by specifying interest areas and topics.
- **Demographic, Location and Language targeting.** Target users on their age, gender, location and language.

Video

Video ads show before or after (and sometimes in the middle of) YouTube videos or video partners on the Google display network. Ads can promote a product or service or can promote video content.

Types of Video Ads

Google offers a range of video ad formats:

- **Skippable In-stream Video Ads.** These are short video ads that play for a minimum of 5 seconds before the user can choose to skip them. They can play before or during the video content.
- **Non-skippable In-stream Video Ads.** These ads can also play right before or during a video but cannot be skipped.
- **Bumper Ads.** Bumper ads are six-second, non-skippable video ads that play before a video.
- **Discovery Ads.** These ads promote your video on the YouTube search results page alongside related videos and the YouTube mobile homepage.
- **Overlays.** Overlay image or text ads on the lower 20% portion of a video.

Fig. 31. YouTube Ad for Wix

Targeting

Before starting a YouTube ad campaign, make sure you have defined the audience you want to reach. Focus on understanding:

- **Demographics.** Define a specific audience based on demographics and language. For example, you could target 28 to 40-year-old new fathers for a baby item.

- **Interests.** You can select viewers searching for specific topics or define the video or channel where ads are shown.
- **Location.** The physical location of your audience, i.e. country, region, city or postcode.

Shopping Ads

Shopping campaigns are product-specific adverts that include detailed product information such as product imagery and price. For retailers, shopping ads account for more than 60% of paid clicks (Source: Search Engine Land[85]).

Shopping ads show in the main search results and under the Shopping tab. Until recently, all shopping results were paid results. Then, in 2020, Google updated their shopping programme to make it more like the standard search results with both free and paid results.

Fig. 32. Google Shopping ads on desktop

---

85   https://searchengineland.com/report-shopping-ads-are-eating-text-ads-accounted-for-60-of-clicks-on-google-33-on-bing-in-q1-297273

Product feeds

When creating Shopping ads, the advertiser does not specify a list of keywords. Instead, the advertiser submits a product 'feed' (a file specifying product details) through Google Merchant Centre[86]. Google then displays these products against relevant searches.

The quality of your product feed (including your product titles, descriptions, images, categories and attributes) is vital for shopping ads for the following reasons:

- **Conversion rate.** The images and title appear in the search results and influence the click-through rate.
- **Search exposure.** Google automatically matches the content of the product feed against search queries. Therefore, thin content will result in less exposure.

It is therefore essential to spend time on the quality of your feed, including:

- **Categorisation.** Google's feed specification has a category tree and each product should have a carefully chosen category.
- **Specifying optional attributes.** Each Google category has a list of optional attributes.
- **Optimised titles.** Ensure that your Google shopping titles include keywords such as brand and size. These may be missing from your website titles.

Product groups

Another difference between shopping and search ads is that Shopping Ads do not use ad groups but instead organise products into 'Product Groups' subdivided to improve targeting.

---

86   https://www.google.com/retail/solutions/merchant-center

Google Shopping tips

Tip 1: If you sell physical goods, Shopping ads are the most effective and easiest way to sell across an extensive catalogue. Performance is usually better than other advertising types, including Search.

Tip 2: By submitting a product feed to Google Merchant Centre, your product will appear in the free results part of Google's shopping results and will generate free traffic for your business.

Improving campaign performance

Google Ads provides information on performance at a target level, so improvements can be made when enough clicks have been collected. Performance can be measured by click-through rate or by conversion data.

If a keyword or other target is underperforming, an advertiser can remove or refine it. Refine the message if you think the target is relevant and should perform better. You can do this by either changing the ad copy or breaking out the keywords into entirely separate ad groups with a more targeted message. Equally, if a keyword performs well, it may be worth separating it into another ad group.

By looking at search data, you may find that your adverts are triggered by searches not relevant to your business. Limit these using keyword matching types, especially negative keywords.

Finally, keyword creation is not a one-off job. As part of ongoing account management, generate relevant keywords and add them to your campaign, both in existing and new ad groups.

Summary

Google Ads are a significant source of paid traffic to most online retailers. Campaigns are mostly charged on a CPC (Cost-Per-Click) basis, which means you only pay for the traffic you get. Advertisers set a daily budget for advertising and there is no minimum spend. Advertisers can define targets (key phrases, pages or products) and matching types to increase the campaign's focus and improve performance.

Campaigns are quick to set up and advertisers can quickly start optimising using performance data. Google's Smart Campaigns utilise machine learning to learn from your campaign's performance and manage campaigns based on your goals.

There is a range of different advertising options which have different uses. These include Shopping Ads for promoting catalogue sales, retargeting ads for enticing back website visitors and textual Search Ads which appear next to Google's general search results. In addition, advertisers can choose whether to target users solely on Google search or other Google sites e.g. YouTube and Gmail. A broad spectrum of internet users can also be reached through Google's Display Network.

Resources

Google has a comprehensive support centre for their advertising products:

Google ads: https://support.google.com/google-ads/?hl=en-GB#topic=10286612

Google merchant centre: https://support.google.com/merchants#topic=7259123

While a lot smaller than Google, Microsoft's Bing search engine also has an advertising programme

https://about.ads.microsoft.com/en-gb/solutions

If you are looking for inspiration for landing pages, HubSpot has published a comprehensive resource of free templates:

https://blog.hubspot.com/marketing/free-landing-page-templates

6:

AFFILIATE MARKETING

Whatever niche you are in, there will be bloggers, influencers and review sites interested in the same area as you. Affiliate marketing allows you to piggyback on these sites and generates much-appreciated income for the partner sites.

At Hello Baby, we run a highly successful affiliate programme through one of the major networks. While much of our traffic comes from larger affiliates (e.g. Cashback and voucher sites), it also gives us a presence on a range of specialist sites. This promotes our brand and drives a significant proportion of our sales.

What is Affiliate Marketing?

Affiliate marketing lets an online retailer (the advertiser) increase sales by allowing others, which target the same audience (known as affiliates or publishers), to earn a commission by recommending their products.

The publisher promotes products by using a unique link. They get paid a commission when a visitor to their site clicks on this link (e.g. a banner, logo or text link), goes to the advertiser's website and performs a particular action. Usually, this is the completion of a transaction such as buying a product or subscribing to a service.

Benefits of Affiliate Marketing

Affiliate marketing is a massive opportunity for all eCommerce businesses. Affiliate marketing is responsible for driving up to 16% of eCommerce sales in the USA (Source: Business Insider[87]). Benefits include:

Targeted traffic

Whatever your product, there will be publishers focused on your niche. Sites such as review sites and blogs can send targeted traffic to your products. For example, to monetise their content, a pram review site might have affiliate links to pram retailers.

Pay on results

Affiliate marketing is a performance marketing channel with payment on completed sales only. This model makes affiliate marketing a low-risk channel that is attractive to merchants. Of course, some affiliates will want to be paid for impressions, but this is much less favourable for the advertiser as it does not directly relate to sales.

Publishers may offer the opportunity to promote offers at an additional cost. Many affiliate networks are free to use, but some will charge a monthly subscription.

Direct

Unlike some channels (e.g. online marketplaces), the merchant can invite people to opt-in to marketing messages after the sale.

---

87   https://www.businessinsider.com/the-affiliate-marketing-report-how-mainstream-publishers-are-turning-performance-based-marketing-into-a-fine-art-2015-11?r=US&IR=T

Low start-up costs

Setting up an affiliate programme through an existing network has limited setup costs.

Boost brand awareness

Consumers like to buy from retailers with whom they are familiar. Affiliate marketing enables companies to grow brand awareness by appearing on multiple contextually relevant sites across the web. For example, a clothing manufacturer could appear on numerous fashion-focused blogs by launching an affiliate scheme and recruiting the right publishers.

Expand internationally

The larger affiliate platforms will have an international presence and enable your brand to reach publishers worldwide.

How Affiliate Marketing works

An advertiser that promotes its products via affiliate marketing is running an affiliate scheme or programme. Some merchants will manage their own programmes and pay affiliates directly. However, most will employ an affiliate network that will handle all the tracking and payments to publishers on their behalf. An affiliate network will also have existing relationships with publishers. This enables them to promote the merchant's programme to their current members and quickly drive referrals.

The advertiser typically only pays on results with affiliate marketing, making it an attractive model for merchants. On top of the commission, some advertisers will offer opportunities to pay for placement on affiliate sites to get additional exposure.

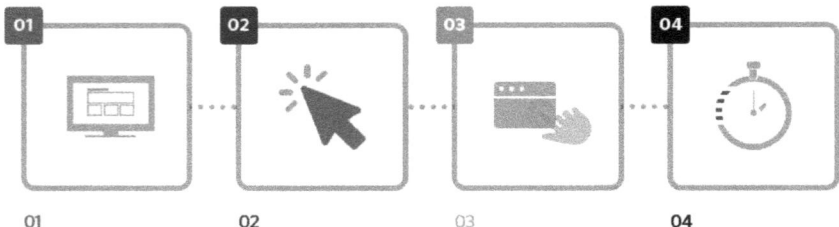

01   02   03   04

Fig. 33. Affiliate marketing process

The process of affiliate marketing is as follows:

1. Potential customer lands on the publisher's website.
2. The Customer clicks an affiliate link and is taken to a landing page detailing the advertiser's product.
3. The Customer buys a product and the tracking software records the purchase data and reports this to the network.
4. The publisher earns a set percentage of the transaction value as a commission.

The affiliate link that the customer clicks upon contains a unique code that identifies the publisher. The affiliate network identifies the transaction using this code and pays out depending on their programme's terms (e.g. 5% of sales, not including shipping).

For example, when purchasing a new bike, a person may research offers on a bike-focused website (e.g. Singletrack). They read a review they like (a 'Giant' bike) and click through to the Giant site to purchase. In this case, Singletrack is the publisher and the advertiser is Giant. Giant would pay Singletrack a commission for generating a sale through their site. If an affiliate network facilitates the programme, they will manage commission and tracking and the advertiser and publisher will not communicate directly.

Tracking

Generally, affiliate programs work on a commission basis where the commission goes to the last publisher site visited before the consumer made the purchase.

To track the sale, the advertising merchant (or the network they work with) gives each affiliate a unique link to record who was responsible for a sale. When a user clicks that link, a file called a cookie is saved on their device. An affiliate cookie does two things:

1. It helps the merchant attribute the sale back to the right publisher.
2. It records the date of the interaction. Typically, publishers will get paid if a sale is made days or weeks after the visit. The advertiser sets this period.

What is an Affiliate Network?

Affiliate networks are services that mediate between the publisher and the advertiser. Advertisers publish their affiliate programs on an affiliate network and publishers can search the network to find programs they wish to promote. An affiliate network manages the relationship between publisher and advertiser, including tracking and payments.

To use the services of a network, advertisers and publishers must first create an account with the network. Once accepted, advertisers can add their programs to the network. Publishers can then apply.

Publishers can apply to any programme in which they wish to participate. Once accepted as an affiliate partner with the advertiser, they have access to a choice of promotional texts or creatives for use on Social Media, emails or websites. The publisher places the affiliate link on their site and when potential customers click on the link, they are taken to the advertiser's website to complete their purchase. The visit is tracked by the affiliate network so that the sale can be attributed to the publisher.

Affiliate networks will typically offer two levels of service:

- **Self-service.** The advertiser will manage their program, including recruiting affiliates and managing commissions.
- **Managed service.** The network will manage the program on the advertiser's behalf, enabling them to employ best practices in running their programs.

Affiliate Network vs direct Affiliate Marketing?

Advertisers can work directly with publishers to promote their products but using an affiliate network is more straightforward and secure.

Benefits of using an affiliate network include:

Managed affiliate solution

Managing an affiliate programme is complex. Affiliate networks streamline the process by providing technology, end-to-end tracking, payment and reporting. This makes it easy to track, monitor and tweak your programme. The larger networks will also have a range of publishers already signed up to their network, ready for an advertiser to onboard.

Program-launch expertise

Working with an established network means publishers are more likely to trust you and your brand. In addition, having systems in place for tracking and payment offers publishers peace of mind that they will get paid.

Affiliate networks that offer account management can support advertisers by providing feedback on performance and benchmarking. They can also suggest campaign ideas and recommendations to help advertisers achieve their objectives.

Approval of publishers

Publishers must apply to join an affiliate network and then request approval for each advertiser program. As not all publishers are accepted, your products are only promoted by publishers the network has decided are good partners for the advertisers on their platform.

Sales tracking and reporting

Affiliate networks should provide you with a comprehensive dashboard that tracks impressions, clicks, conversions, sales and revenue and generates reports. You can monitor which publishers and campaigns generate the most sales, allowing you to optimize your affiliate marketing.

Types of publishers

A publisher is an individual or company that earns a commission from promoting an advertiser's products or services. This may be through links in the copy on websites such as blogs or articles, Social Media posts, newsletters or clickable banners or images.

The most common publishing types are:

Bloggers and Content Sites

Bloggers and content sites (e.g. review sites, online newspapers) build up an audience by writing engaging and informative content. Affiliate marketing is one of the ways they monetise their content and audience. They may promote affiliate products directly within their content or alongside it. An example of a site supported by affiliate income is PCMag.

Offers, cashback and coupon sites

Consumers love discounts and merchants can use this to their advantage by distributing their deals on offer sites. These websites then drive traffic to the offer on the advertiser's site.

Offer websites include:

- **Voucher/coupon sites.** These sites list codes by brand and type. Examples include my voucher codes[88] and voucher cloud[89].
- **Cashback sites.** These sites pay out all or most of the affiliate commissions they receive to their members. They also list codes that can be used in conjunction with the cashback. Examples: Quidco[90], Topcashback[91].
- **Apps and browser extensions.** These help consumers quickly find discounts while shopping, e.g. camel camel[92], Honey[93].
- **Social Media and blogs.** Sites related to discussing discount codes.

Tip: These sites are the biggest affiliates across most sectors, so make sure you are on the major players.

---

88   https://www.myvouchercodes.co.uk
89   https://www.vouchercloud.com
90   https://www.quidco.com
91   https://www.topcashback.co.uk
92   https://camelcamelcamel.com
93   https://www.joinhoney.com

Shopping comparison sites

Shopping comparison sites were popular in the noughties but most disappeared when Google moved into this space. The ones who remain make some or all their revenue through affiliate schemes. Examples: Pricesearcher[94], PriceSpy[95].

Email marketing

Some publishing businesses have built up large email marketing lists which they contact regularly. The emails will be a mixture of helpful content and promotions. Emailers work hard to build trust and authority with their subscribers, so purchase rates tend to be high when they recommend a product.

An example organisation that has built up an extensive, targeted list is Bounty[56]. Bounty provides new parents with a hospital gift pack with samples from various brands. Alongside the pack, parents can sign up for Bounty's newsletter, which has tens of thousands of subscribers.

Social Media influencers

Influencers are users on Social Media platforms such as Instagram, YouTube, Facebook, TikTok and Twitter who have built up a substantial following. Whilst high-profile influencers can demand hefty upfront fees for promoting products, others will earn additional income through affiliate commissions.

Tip: You can approach influencers directly and make them aware of your programme and how they can benefit.

---

94   https://www.pricesearcher.com

95   https://pricespy.co.uk

96   https://www.bounty.com

Commission and other fees

Advertisers set commission rates, which vary widely depending on the product and the sector. For example, electrical retailers will be as low as 1 or 2%, whilst retailers selling virtual products may offer 50% or more. Advertisers can create multiple programs that offer different commissions based on performance or other factors. For example:

- 5% on branded products but 10% on own-branded products.
- 5% standard commission but 10% for a popular voucher site to get better placement.
- 10% on non-sale products but only 5% on sale products.
- 10% standard commission but only 5% if a voucher is used.

A higher commission level will attract affiliates and lead to more promotion. On top of the commission, the affiliate network may charge a monthly management fee and a commission 'override.' The override is typically 20-30%.

Creating an Affiliate Programme

Analyse the competition
Before starting an affiliate program, it is good to analyse what your competitors are doing. The competitive environment will help you set commissions, promotions and objectives.

Decide on the goal for your programme
Setting clear goals for your programme will help you identify the affiliates you wish to recruit. An affiliate marketing programme should consist of a balanced mix of affiliate partners.

Short-term or Long-term?

If the campaign's goal is short-term, e.g. launching a new product or promoting a sale, it might be best to create a high-incentive campaign that will attract many affiliates and drive traffic fast. On the other hand, if the goal is longer-term, such as launching in a fresh territory or expanding your customer base, you will need to partner with sites to which shoppers continually return.

Who is the target customer?

Think about how your target customer shops, e.g. what sites they read and emails to which they subscribe. Select affiliates that specialise in your business area and attract your target customer.

What is your goal?

What is the purpose of the program? Are you trying to boost revenue? Do you want newsletter subscribers? How much do you want to spend to acquire a customer?

Some common goals that you might have for your program could be:

- To increase the sales volume by 5% year-on-year.
- To increase the sales value by 10% month-on-month.
- To increase the average order value by £20.
- To increase the number of active affiliates in the program by 30% by the end of the year.

Choosing an Affiliate Network

Many affiliate networks are available and the same publisher site may well be on several affiliate networks. Consider the following when selecting a network:

- **Fees and agreements.** Some networks will want to charge a monthly fee, whilst others will be free. Also, be wary of entering into long-term contracts. A 30-day notice period is usually plenty.

- **Relevant publishers.** Publishers with an established affiliate business are likely to work with specific affiliate networks and may be reluctant to join another just to work with you. Therefore, request a list of affiliates relevant to your business from each network.
- **Other publishers.** Avoid networks that have publishers with whom you would not want to be associated (e.g. gambling), as your brand may end up alongside these. Consider whether the network works with any large brand which will attract high-quality publishers.
- **Reporting.** What is the quality of the reporting available? Can you drill down to see where the traffic and sales are originating?
- **Support.** What level of support will you receive? For example, will you have a dedicated account manager?

One frequent mistake is to think that you should look elsewhere if your competitors are on a network. On the contrary, the presence of competitors may be a good thing as they may well be there because this is the best source of affiliates.

Create collateral for publishers

Some publishers will require content to help promote your business to their audience. Therefore, when inviting publishers to join your campaign, it is best to provide as much material as possible. Content includes logos, digital banners and videos of your products.

You should consider creating bespoke content for your top affiliates so they can better promote your products. Influencers (e.g. bloggers, Instagrammers) must constantly create content to keep their sites fresh. By creating content for their use, you will get extra promotion for your products and form stronger bonds with your publishers.

Recruit publishers

Once you have created your programme, it is time to recruit publishers. Your aim should be to get the publishers on board who have an audience that matches your target customer. Affiliate networks will have a browsable list of affiliates. You should also get a list of suitable publishers when you onboard to a new network.

Monitor results

Once you have your affiliate programme up and running, you need to measure your progress against your set goals. For this, decide what Key Performance Indicators (KPIs) you will be using. Some KPIs will be sales-related; however, as your campaign's health depends on recruiting and retaining good affiliates, you should also monitor metrics that cover the quality and quantity of the affiliates signed up to your programme.

Commonly used KPIs include:

Affiliate traffic

Monitor trends in your affiliate traffic over time and compare them to your other sales channels. If your affiliate traffic is declining, it is time to engage with your current affiliates and recruit new ones. Declining affiliate traffic may be because other advertisers offer better commission or your website is not converting. Ensure that your affiliates have enough incentive to promote your products.

Revenue from affiliates

Revenue is a measure of the overall impact of your affiliate programme on your business. If revenue is declining, this could be due to a drop in traffic (see above). Alternatively, the site conversion rate could be problematic if traffic is unchanged but revenue is down.

Percentage of active affiliates

An active affiliate is one that generates sales within a set period (as decided by the advertiser). This measure provides valuable feedback on the quality of your affiliates. If only a fraction of your affiliates are active, it is time to re-evaluate your affiliate recruitment strategy. It may be that you are not targeting the right segments.

Note: Before measuring this metric, you must decide what you consider an 'active' affiliate. This is defined as an affiliate who generate x sales in y period, e.g. one sale in three months.

Summary

Affiliate marketing helps merchants reach their target audience by connecting with consumers through a wide range of niche publishing sites. The publisher will use a unique link to direct consumers to the advertiser's site. The publisher will get paid if this link is clicked and a sale or other conversion event is recorded. Affiliate schemes normally run on a commission basis, so this channel is minimal risk.

Most retailers will run their affiliate programme through an Affiliate Network. Affiliate networks, such as Commission Junction[97], manage tracking orders and affiliate payment. This takes the pain out of running a scheme. The larger networks will also have many publishers already signed up and this allows advertisers to get a programme up and running quickly.

---

97   https://www.cj.com

7:

EMAIL MARKETING

Switching suppliers is only a Google search away. If you do not encourage repeat business, your customers will go elsewhere. Your return customer rate can be the difference between a failing and a thriving business and recruiting new customers is expensive.

Staying in touch with past customers via email is a highly effective strategy for encouraging repeat purchases and building your brand. It is also a low-cost way to build relations with past customers or even browsers who never followed through on a purchase. Emails can send transactional, promotional, informative and sales lifecycle messages.

Why Email Marketing is important

Unless you have a strategy for promoting repeat purchases, most new customers will buy once and never return. Building an email list and sending compelling email campaigns gives you a way to retain your hard-won customers as it provides subscribers with a reason to stay in touch.

If your eCommerce business has not invested in email marketing, you are certainly losing sales by missing potential customers.

Email marketing has the following advantages for eCommerce businesses:

Drives repeat business

Return customers are essential for eCommerce businesses because they keep the cost of sales down. Search engines and Social Media are great for recruiting new customers. However, email plays a pivotal role in encouraging the second purchase and beyond once a customer is acquired.

Effective sales channel

Research from the leading eCommerce platform Shopify[98] shows that email traffic had the highest order conversion rate during peak periods. Additionally, 80% of businesses rely on email as their primary channel for acquisition and retention (source Emarsys[99]).

Improves sales performance

There are only three ways to improve revenue: increasing the total number of customers, increasing the total number of purchases per customer and increasing the average order value (AOV). Email can improve performance in all three areas:

- Automated welcome and abandoned cart emails can boost conversion rates.
- Win-back campaigns increase the number of purchases a customer makes.
- Lifecycle campaigns and promotions can automatically highlight high-value products to targeted customers, increasing AOV.

---

98   https://www.shopify.co.uk/blog/email-marketing#benefits

99   https://emarsys.com/learn/white-papers/adapting-to-the-pace-of-omnichannel-commerce

As your email marketing campaign matures, your list will grow and performance will improve. Therefore, it is never too soon to start email marketing.

Full control

Platforms such as Amazon, Google and Facebook are growing in importance for online retailers. However, whilst these platforms are a vital part of the marketing mix for any eCommerce business, they have serious disadvantages:

- **Charges.** To acquire customers through platforms requires payment, either on a commission (e.g. eBay or Amazon) or advertising charge (e.g. Google).
- **You do not own the customer.** You do not own the customer with marketplace platforms and cannot market directly to them.
- **Potential for exclusion.** If you break the platform's rules for actual or perceived infringements, you can get barred either temporarily or permanently.

With email, you own the customers and the cost of running an email campaign is low (price of email system and any promotions).

Running an Email Marketing campaign

Unless you have a tiny email list, sending an email marketing campaign requires specialist email marketing software. You will also need a strategy for building your list in a way that does not alienate your customers or break the law.

Choosing Email Marketing software

Email marketing software is a dedicated software tool for managing email marketing campaigns. Many are on the market, such as Mailchimp[100] and Klaviyo[101] and you can always change provider later.

Functionality includes:

- **List building.** Forms for collecting email addresses.
- **List management.** Managing lists, including unsubscribe requests.
- **Broadcasts.** Email campaigns sent to all or a segment of your list.
- **Flows.** Rule-based automatic emails.
- **Analytics.** Reporting on your email campaign performance.

As an online retailer, you should use a system that specialises in eCommerce.

Factors to consider include:

- **Cost.** Email software is usually charged by the number of names in your list or the number of outgoing emails.
- **Usability.** The system should enable you to create emails and highly configurable flows without coding.
- **Integration.** Choose a system that integrates with your current eCommerce system. This will enable you to push customer data directly into your email, allowing for a more personalised experience.

---

100   https://mailchimp.com
101   https://www.klaviyo.com

Building an email list

Businesses should take all opportunities to build their email list. The larger your list, broadly speaking, the more business it will generate. In addition, as users subscribe to receive emails from your website and verify their identity by clicking on a link (double opt-in), they are interested in what you have to offer and are more likely to convert into paying customers.

Customer opt-in

You need permission to add email addresses to your list, not just from a marketing standpoint but also legally. Receiving unsolicited marketing emails (i.e. spam) is annoying for customers and, in many places, against the law. To give consent to be contacted, subscribers need to 'opt-in' to receive marketing messages from you. Permission is usually obtained by ticking a box at checkout.

A business that neglects its legal obligations can get heavily fined. To avoid this fate, you should consult the relevant legislation, some of which is shown below:

- **CAN-SPAM**[102]. Controlling the Assault of Non-Solicited Pornography and Marketing Act of 2003 governs email usage for commercial purposes in the US.
- **GDPR**[103]. The General Data Protection Regulation is legislation aimed at protecting personal data within the European Union.
- **UK GDPR**[104]. After Brexit, the UK has its own set of GDPR rules.

---

102 https://www.ftc.gov/tips-advice/business-center/guidance/can-spam-act-compliance-guide-business

103 https://gdpr-info.eu

104 https://ico.org.uk/for-organisations/guide-to-data-protection/guide-to-the-general-data-protection-regulation-gdpr

- **CASL**[105]. Canadian Anti-Spam Legislation sets out the regulations for communicating with Canadian customers.

Opt-in forms

You must ask to get people to sign up for your newsletter. There are several places on your website to request users to subscribe. Visitors to your website are likely interested in your products and within your target market. Therefore, asking for a subscription can have a reasonable response rate, especially if you provide an incentive to sign up, e.g. a first-time customer discount.

The following are popular methods for implementing forms:

- **Tick box at checkout.** Invite customers to sign up as part of the checkout process. Pre-ticking the box will increase sign-ups but it is sneaky and against the law in many countries.
- **Sign up box.** This can be in the header, navigation or footer. Although the conversion rate is likely to be low, the subscribers will add up over time.
- **Pop-up box.** Pops-ups can be triggered after a specific time or by signs the customer is leaving. A signup incentive may encourage them to make a purchase.

Signup incentives

Unfortunately, 'please sign up to our newsletter' is frequently not enough incentive for a customer to bother subscribing. However, creating an offer can incentivise visitors to share their email addresses.

Options include:

- **Deals and discounts.** Discounts are a double-edged sword as they increase sales but hit margins. It is a judgment call

---

105   https://fightspam.gc.ca/eic/site/030.nsf/eng/home

whether it encourages customers who would purchase in any case.

- **Competition or contest.** Although contests can generate many signups, many entrants will be just looking for free stuff (a 'comper').
- **Educational content.** Many products benefit from sharing additional content with customers. For example, to encourage repeat purchases, a food manufacturer could email tasty recipes that utilise their product.

Real-world email requests

Emails can be collected where you physically interact with your customers. Examples include:

- **Physical stores.** If you have a shop, you can ask customers to sign up at checkout or, to collect contact details, give an incentive such as a competition.
- **Packaging inserts.** These can include discounts or offers for customers who return to your site.

Types of email marketing campaigns

There are three main types of eCommerce emails: transactional, promotional and lifecycle emails.

- **Transactional emails.** These are functional emails that, as part of the purchasing process, send order information to individual customers. Emails include order confirmation and reviews emails.
- **Promotional emails.** Promotional emails advertise a specific deal or promotion. This can be across the whole product range or just a subset, e.g. Black Friday or Cyber Monday email offers.

- **Lifecycle emails.** Lifecycle emails are also known as automations or 'triggered' emails. This is because they are sent based on the user's action or where the user is in the customer lifecycle. For example, an abandoned cart email is sent after a customer leaves products in their cart for a specific time without paying.

Transactional emails

Transactional emails may be functional, but they have an extremely high open rate. The average unique open rate for transactional emails is over 47%, more than twice the 22% open rate for non-transactional emails (Source: IBM[106]). Transactional emails also have a much higher click-through rate of 9% versus 3% for non-transactional emails.

Due to their high engagement rate, these emails are an excellent opportunity to promote your business. They should be well-crafted and contain carefully targeted marketing messages. Options include:

- **Products upsell.** Suggest accessories or add the option for subscription purchase.
- **Promotional codes.** Offer a time-limited incentive for a second purchase. This is known as a bounce-back offer.
- **Get Social.** Invite your customers to a Facebook group or ask them to follow your Social Media accounts.

Other ideas for improving your order processing emails include:

- **Order tracking.** Include a direct link to the order progress, including any tracking details. Good communication

---

106 https://digiday.com/wp-content/uploads/2016/07/Email-Marketing-Metrics-Benchmark-Study-2016-IBM.pdf

reassures buyers and cuts down on customer service queries.

- **Refer a friend.** Encourage word-of-mouth marketing by implementing a referral program with rewards.
- **Relevant product suggestions.** Suggest products that complement a customer's purchase.

Note: In the EU and the UK, under GDPR, promotional messages are not permitted in transactional emails. Transactional emails are one-to-one emails (i.e. they are sent directly to the customer) triggered by a transaction or user activity. Examples include order confirmation, order dispatch or password change emails.

Merchant and product reviews

Customer feedback was pioneered by marketplaces such as eBay. It is now available to standalone websites using services such as Reviews[107], Trustpilot[108] and Feefo[109]. Collecting feedback is an excellent way to reassure customers that you are a reputable business.

Only request feedback once a customer has had time to receive and use their product. The services above are third-party apps that collect user experience details. This is a convenient solution for feedback collection. However, placing the review or survey on your site offers more opportunities for upselling to the customer.

If you collect feedback, it is vital to monitor it and deal with unhappy customers.

---

107 https://www.reviews.io
108 https://www.trustpilot.com
109 https://www.feefo.com

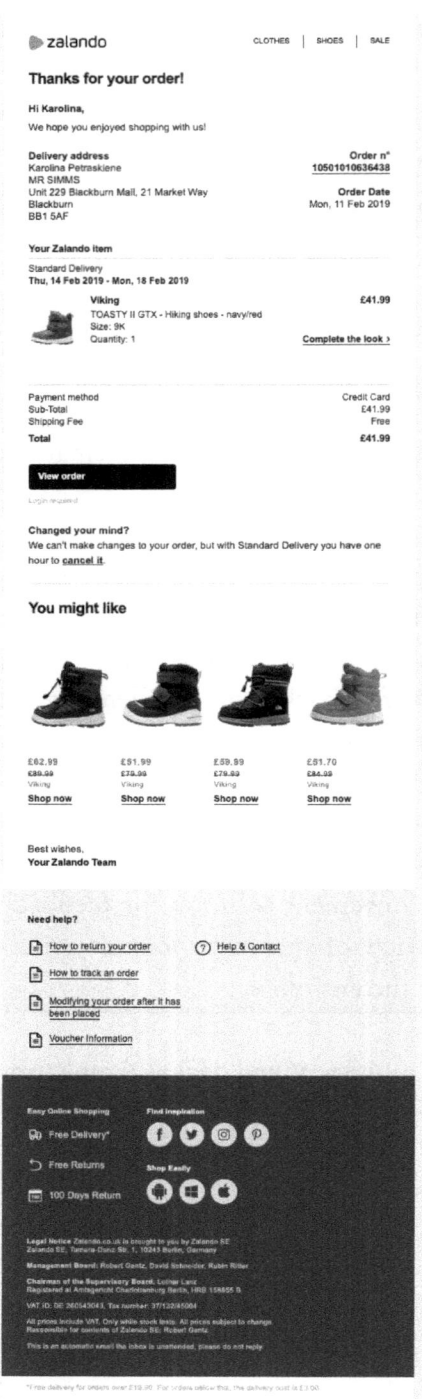

Fig. 34. Zalando order confirmation email featuring order info, upsell and social links.

Promotional emails

Promotional emails are sent to all or part of your email subscriber list. Sending to part of your subscriber list is referred to as segmenting. Examples of promotional emails include a new product launch, email newsletters, time-limited offers or seasonal promotions. For maximum impact when sending a promotional email, you should carefully target the content to the subscriber segment to which you are sending.

Types of promotional email include:

New product launches

Customers love newness! When launching a new product or range of products, you could send the details to a segment of customers who have purchased related products in the past.

Time-sensitive offers

Everyone loves a deal, so a successful strategy is to send time-limited offers to customers who have shown interest in these products in the past.

Exclusive subscriber discounts

If you send out a regular newsletter, give readers a reason to stay subscribed by offering exclusive discounts and offers. Email-only offers are a terrific way to keep subscribers interested and build loyalty.

Seasonal promotions

A tried and tested form of email marketing is running exclusive offers based on upcoming events and holidays. Examples include a Black Friday sale, a January sale or Fathers' Day.

Newsletter

A regular newsletter can educate your customers and reinforce your brand. Distributing informative content such as customer case studies and articles is a way of contacting customers without relying on discounts or promotions. For example, the following from Amazon lets customers know that Black Friday is on its way and this email is an invitation to visit the store and get buying.

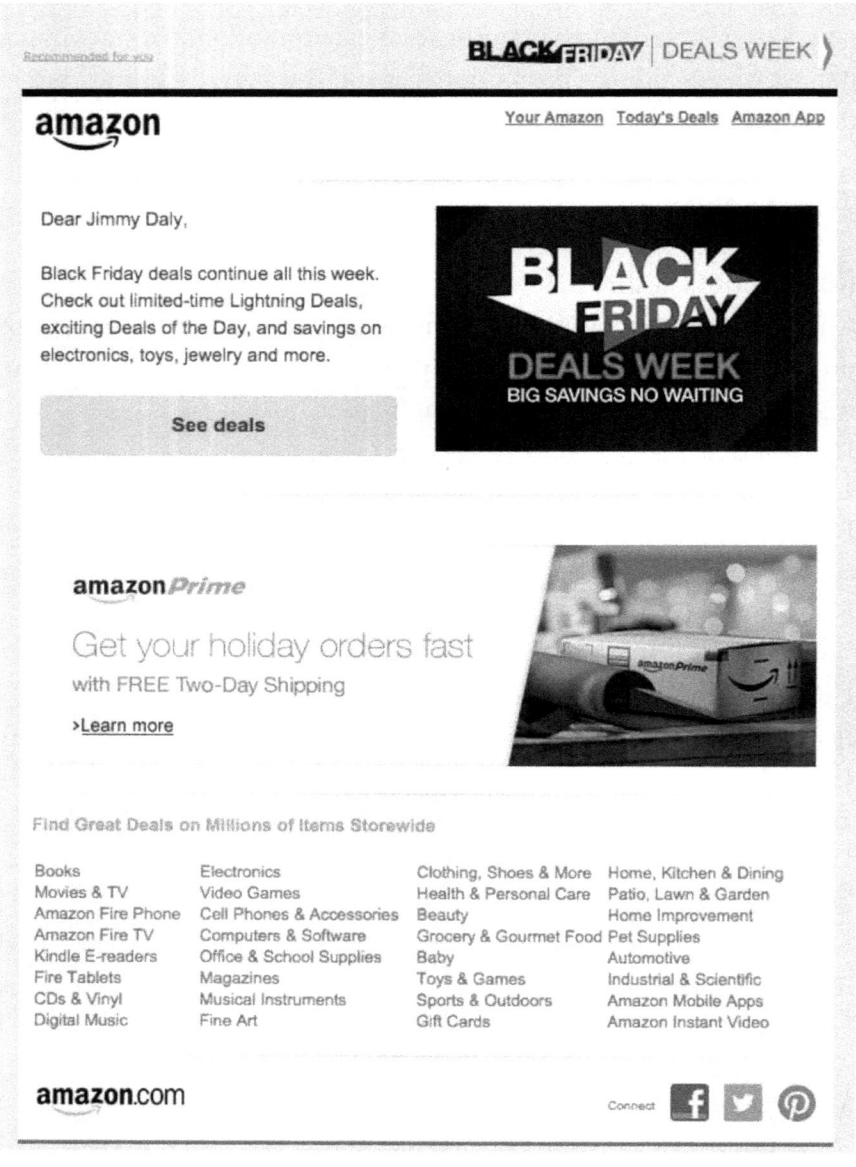

Fig. 35. Black Friday Deal email from Amazon

Lifecycle emails

Lifecycle emails target a small segment of your subscribers with relevant messages based on their behaviour. Their targeted nature means they can include a carefully tailored message to improve engagement.

Effective lifecycle emails include abandoned cart, welcome series, second order and win-back emails. Based on triggering events. These emails can be configured in your email marketing software to be sent out automatically. The sending sequence of these emails is referred to as a 'flow'.

Abandoned cart

An abandoned cart occurs when a product is added to a cart, but the customer never completes the purchase. About 60-80% of shopping carts are abandoned, which is a lot of lost sales.

Abandoned cart emails are automatic messages sent to these website visitors to remind them to complete the purchase. These emails typically recover between 5-11% of missed sales, which is a straightforward way to boost revenue. To improve conversion, many retailers include offers, though this can encourage shoppers to abandon their carts to get a discount.

Welcome series

Welcome emails are a series of emails sent to customers after they subscribe to an email list. The purpose of these emails is to welcome customers to the brand and build a long-term relationship (starting with a second purchase).

Welcome series emails have a high average open rate of 45%, which is highly effective (Source: Omnisend[110]). In addition, first purchase

---

[110] https://www.omnisend.com/blog/email-marketing-automation

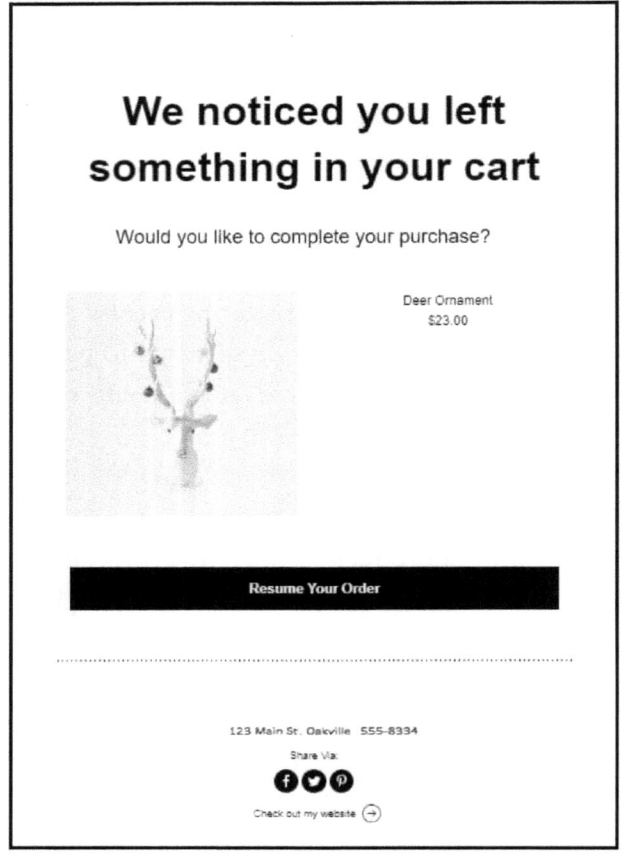

Fig. 36. A simple yet effective abandoned cart email.

automation produces 3-6 times more sales than regular promotional emails.

A three email welcome series might look something like this:

- **1st Email – Encourage purchase.** Say hello and thank them, with a 10% discount voucher, for subscribing to the newsletter.
- **2nd – Email – Build a relationship.** Invite the subscribers to connect on Social Media to learn more about the brand.
- **3rd Email – Re-engage and drive traffic back to the store.** Send a reminder to customers who have not yet purchased that there is a discount waiting for them.

In the example below, soap-maker Lush highlights their products with fantastic imagery and product showcase. Recommending products from the start drives traffic back to the site to get people shopping again.

Welcome emails should be sent shortly after sign-up (especially if you offer a sign-up bonus) and include a clear call to action. In addition, the emails should provide value upfront (e.g. discount, promotions) as you only have a brief time to make a good impression.

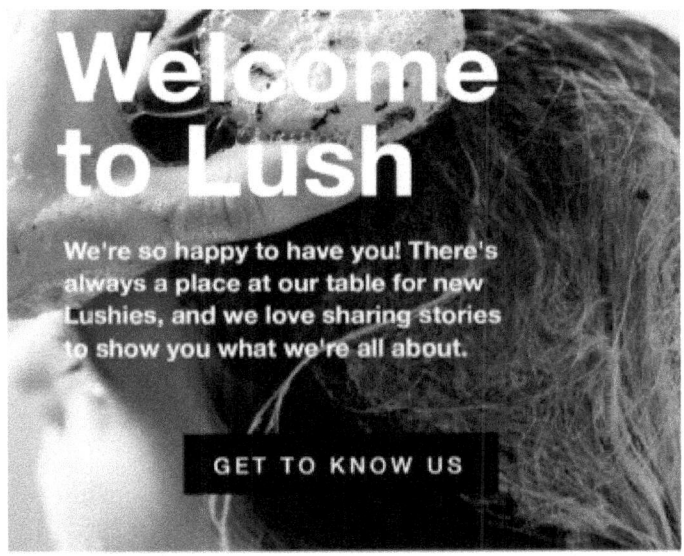

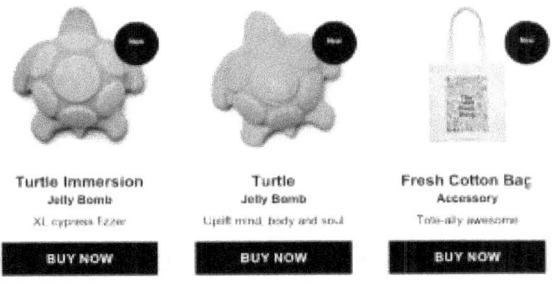

Fig 37. Lush welcome email

Second-order campaign

Unless you take active steps to get them back to your site, most customers will buy only one product and then go elsewhere. A second-order campaign aims to get single-order customers to return to the site by highlighting complementary products they might want to buy.

These emails increase customer lifetime value and reduce the number of customers going to a competitor for their add-on purchases. For example, eCommerce leader Amazon gets 35% of its business from follow up emails (Source: McKinsey[111]).

Win-back series

Win-back email campaigns encourage lapsed customers back to the site. For example, if you know that 90% of customers who make a second purchase do so within 45 days, you could send out a targeted offer after that time to entice them back.

Improving performance

Personalisation

Creating a personalised email for each recipient can boost email open rates, click-through and deliverability. Your email software should make importing customer data from your list easy to give each email a distinctive touch.

Optimise for mobile

With the rise of Smartphones, the majority (51%) of emails are opened on a mobile device (Source Return Path112). Make your email easy

---

111 https://www.mckinsey.com/industries/retail/our-insights/how-retailers-can-keep-up-with-consumers

112 https://returnpath.com/downloads/email-client-experience

to read on mobile devices by using a 'responsive' design that adjusts to the size of the viewing device. Before subscribing, check that your email software provider supports responsive designs.

Segmentation

Once you have built an email database, segment it into more specific groupings to send them targeted campaigns. For example, you should send different emails to customers at various buying cycle stages.

Successful segmentation will lead to fewer unsubscribes, a higher click-through rate and increased engagement as users are sent more relevant content.

A/B testing

If you send out a large email campaign, you should perfect the content before sending it. A/B testing allows email variations to be trialled on subsets of users (Groups A and B) before sending the message to the main group of users (Group C). After sending the variations, your email service provider should then tell you which performed the best according to your chosen metrics.

A/B testing can be run on all aspects of an email, including subject line, content and offer type (e.g. fixed amount or percentage discount).

Measuring performance: Email Marketing metrics

Before launching an email marketing campaign, it is essential to understand your goals to know if your campaign is successful. Several key email marketing metrics can help you benchmark the performance of your campaigns.

List size and growth

The more email addresses collected from customers or captured from website visitors, the more extensive your email database and, to grow sales, the more potential customers you can reach. Your email service provider should enable you to monitor this vital metric so you can see how many new subscribers are added on a weekly or monthly basis.

Open rates

The open rate is the percentage of recipients who opened the emails they received. The average rate varies by sector but is around 15-25% (Source: Campaign Monitor[113]). The following factors influence the rate:

- **Subject line.** The subject line, along with the preheader text and the sender's name, is the first thing your recipients will see when they receive an email. It must be compelling.
- **Preview text.** Most email clients show preheader text next to the subject line. With most email service providers, you can edit the preheader text to control the preview content seen by readers.
- **Deliver relevant content.** If your open rate is below average, you may be delivering the wrong content to the wrong people.

Click-Through-Rate (CTR)

The click-through rate measures how many opened emails received at least one click through to the target website. The average click-through rate is 2-3% (source: Campaign Monitor). This should be higher than your average website conversion rate as the email recipients have opted to see your content (e.g. past website customers).

CTR is a measure of how engaging your email content is. The email content, including images and calls to action, obviously plays a

---

113 https://www.campaignmonitor.com/resources/guides/email-marketing-benchmarks

significant role in performance. If your open rate is reasonable, but your CTR is low, the content is underperforming. A/B testing can be used to optimise the click-through rate.

Deliverability

Email deliverability refers to the proportion of emails that end up in the recipient's inbox instead of bouncing or being classified as spam. When mailbox providers receive an email, they will run reputation checks to decide whether the message is SPAM. They make this decision by analysing the historical performance of the sending email address, the domain and the email's content.

Factors considered will include:

- The reputation of the server or IP address used to dispatch the email.
- Domain reputation of links in the content.
- Email bounce rates.
- Spam complaint rates for the sender, domain and server.

To keep the email deliverability high, it is essential to have a good sender reputation. Achieve this by keeping your list up to date. This involves:

- **Removing old emails.** If an email has not interacted well in a long time, consider removing it. Also, remove any emails that bounce.
- **Opted-in subscribers only.** Only send emails to subscribers who have given specific contact permission.
- **Quality content.** Avoid the use of spammy titles, e.g. GET RICH QUICK.
- **Unsubscribe option.** Always include a clear unsubscribe option.

Be careful, as many email service providers consider a 0.1% complaint rate the maximum acceptable threshold.

Revenue

The goal of most email marketing is to drive sales. If email marketing is working well for your business, a reasonable goal is 20% of your sales coming from this channel.

Benchmarking

While the performance of email marketing is individual to each business, an eCommerce business whose email marketing is going well might look like this:

- **20% open rate.** This indicates that you send relevant emails, with interesting subject lines, to the right people
- **5% click-through rate.** This suggests that the content and offers in your emails are compelling enough to click.
- **20% of website revenue from email marketing.** Email marketing converts new customers and upsells enough to existing customers to justify further investment.

Summary

Email marketing is one of the best ways to increase customer loyalty and stay in touch with your customers. In addition, sending emails is inexpensive, so it has an extremely high return on investment and helps keep your sale costs down. This boosts your bottom line. Research has shown that, on average, £1 invested in email marketing generates £38 in sales[114].

---

114 https://www.emailmonday.com/dma-national-client-email-report-2015

With the growth of Social Media, many have forecast the death of email marketing. However, the number of email users is still growing and is estimated to be over 4.2 billion in 2022[115]. Furthermore, users will visit their inbox several times a day. Customised emails are highly personal and targeted and help businesses form strong bonds with their customers. Finally, unlike other forms of marketing (e.g. marketplaces), you own your email list. Firms with a longer email list can obtain higher valuations.

---

115 https://www.statista.com/statistics/255080/number-of-e-mail-users-worldwide

8:

SOCIAL MEDIA

Social media platforms have grown explosively in the last few years. The figures are astonishing:

- 3.8 billion Social Media users across all platforms in 2020 (total world population is 7.7 billion) (Source: We Are Social[116]).
- Facebook has over 2.8 billion active monthly users (Source: Statista[117]).
- Social Commerce is predicted to rise to $604.5 billion by 2027 (Source: Research & Markets[118]).

With billions of users worldwide, it is safe to say that most of your customers will be on one Social Media platform or another. They interact on social channels with their friends, colleagues and brands, looking for entertainment, inspiration, information and recommendations.

---

116   https://wearesocial.com/digital-2020

117   https://www.statista.com/statistics/264810/number-of-monthly-active-facebook-users-worldwide

118   https://www.prnewswire.com/news-releases/assessment-of-the-social-commerce-industry-2020-2027-and-impact-of-covid-19---mobiles-segment-readjusted-to-a-revised-39-2-cagr-for-the-next-7-year-period-301125465.html

At my online retailing company, Hello Baby, we find Social Media is a great way to interact with customers more informally and share fun content about our company. We also find that customers increasingly wish to contact us through social platforms instead of traditional channels like email and phone.

Why your business should be on Social Media

Despite its enormous popularity, many businesses do not use Social Media or only have a minimal presence. This is a big mistake! If your business is not part of the conversation, one of your competitors will be.

Social media can be used for communicating with customers, building your brand and driving sales in the following ways:

- **Customer service.** Customers expect to contact businesses through their Social Media presence, notably Facebook Messenger.
- **Sharing content.** Share content related to your business and fun stuff that you think your audience will enjoy. Urge them to share it with others.
- **Sharing offers.** Sharing selected offers with your customers can help drive sales.
- **Shopping.** Facebook and Instagram now offer a shopfront that links to an eCommerce website. Soon, this will develop into a fully-fledged marketplace.
- **Advertising.** All the significant platforms offer advertising programs. These enable businesses to create super-targeted adverts.

Social media is an opportunity to form closer bonds with customers and differentiate yourself from the competition. However, as many companies' Social Media 'gaffes' have shown, Social Media does require careful management and monitoring.

Businesses can be built or destroyed overnight by Social Media. A single post from a user with a large following (an 'influencer') can drive a massive sales volume. Conversely, a poor piece of customer service that goes viral on Social Media can cause a company's share price to plummet. For example:

- The Cambridge Satchel company's sales were transformed when Taylor Swift wore one of its products[119].
- A (hilarious) song posted on YouTube about poor customer service wiped 10% off United Airlines' share price[120].

The major social networks

The biggest social networks have billions of users all over the world.

These users are not just using the platform once a day but visiting multiple times:

Customer service on Social Media

Social Customer Service provides consumer support through Social Media channels like Facebook and Twitter. 69% of customers believe fast resolution of problems is vital to good service so social consumer support is essential. This is the first port of call for many consumers (source: Zendesk[121]).

---

119 https://www.cambridge-news.co.uk/business/business-news/how-cambridge-satchel-company-changed-15524421
120 https://en.wikipedia.org/wiki/United_Breaks_Guitars
121 https://www.zendesk.co.uk/blog/customer-service-through-social-media

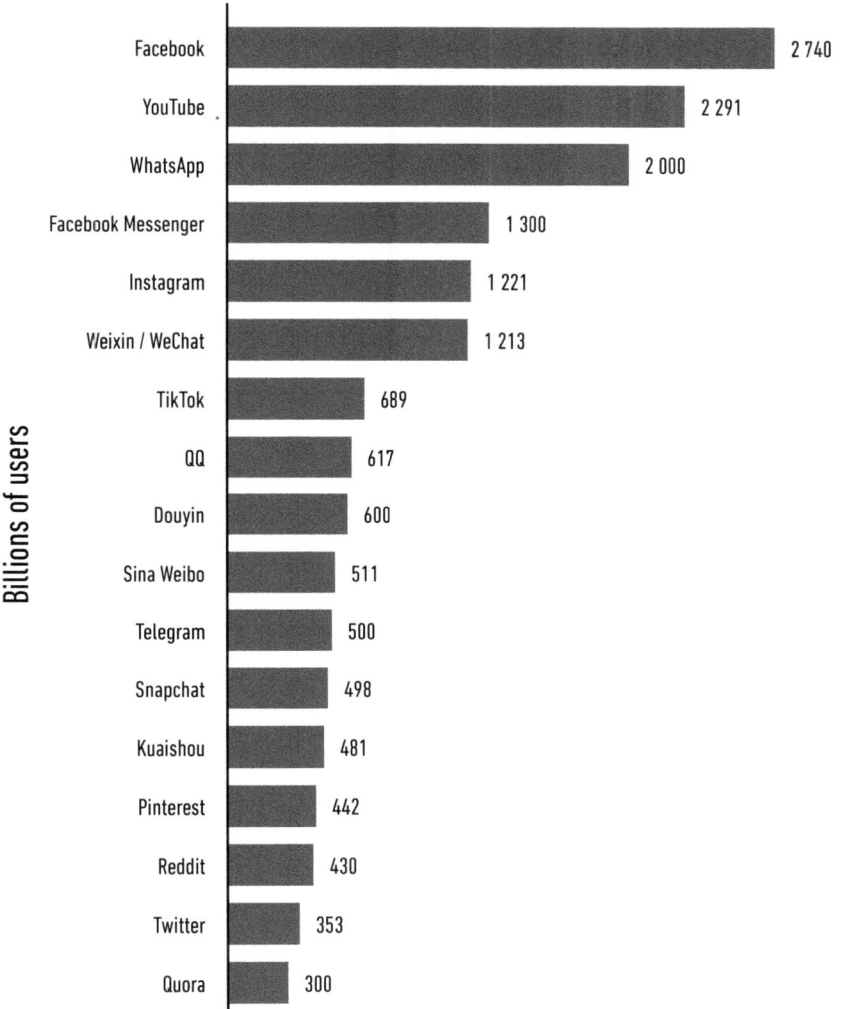

Fig. 37. Major social networks – billions of users
Source: Statista[122]

Platforms such as Facebook, Instagram and Twitter have developed into vital communication channels for brands. They are also channels through which consumers request and receive customer service.

---

122 https://www.statista.com/statistics/272014/global-social-networks-ranked-by-number-of-users

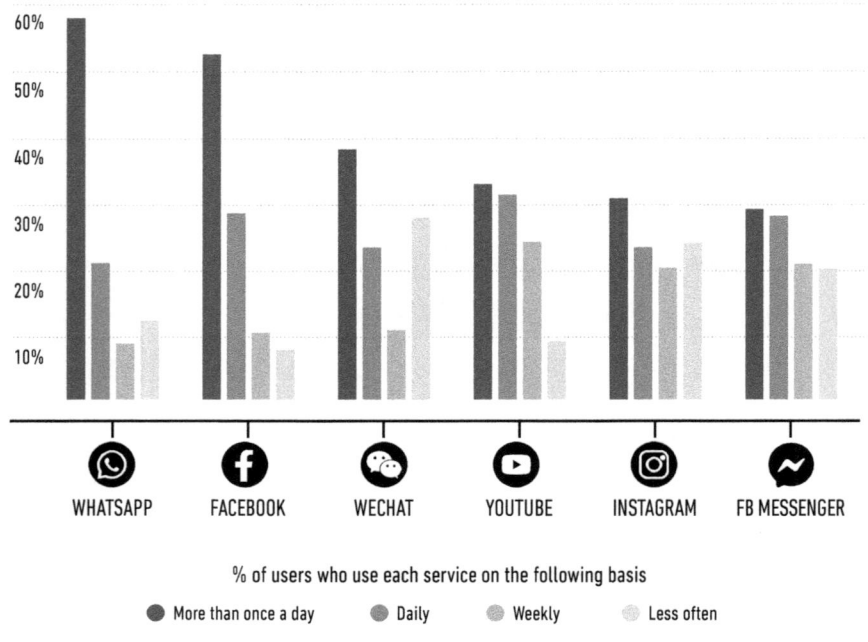

Fig. 38. Social Media usage. Source: Our Social Times[123]

About 90% of consumers have used Social Media in some way to communicate with a brand (source: Sprout Social[124]). Over one third said they preferred Social Media to traditional contact methods such as phone and email.

I recommend frequent monitoring of messages on your Social Media channels and integrating these queries within your customer service system. In a few years, I predict that most customer service queries will go through Social Media platforms, especially messaging apps like WhatsApp.

---

123   https://oursocialtimes.com/7-social-media-statistics-for-2017

124   https://sproutsocial.com/insights/data/q2-2016

Social media marketing

Social media marketing is the practice of creating content that promotes your company and products on Social Media platforms such as Facebook, Twitter and Instagram. It is all about connecting with your target audience and customers where they are socially interacting with each other and your brand.

Your Social Media strategy will depend on which platform your audience frequents. To increase conversions and brand awareness, you should create unique content tailored to the specific network where it is shared. I discuss ideas for good Social Media posts below.

Advertising on Social Media is massive and all the major platforms offer advertising programmes. The most significant player is Facebook which sits, alongside Google, as one of the largest advertising platforms in the world.

Benefits of Social Media marketing

Social Media Marketing can have the following benefits for your business:

Brand awareness

Due to the enormous numbers of people using Social Media, content posted by your business has the potential to reach a massive audience. In addition, posting content can boost brand awareness by improving engagement. Social engagement includes actions like commenting, liking, sharing and re-posting.

Driving website traffic

Social media also increases brand awareness by driving traffic directly to your site. This is done by including direct links to your website in your profile and posts.

Social commerce

Facebook and Instagram both offer a customisable online store. These allow your visitors and followers to view products you have shared in posts. From there, visitors can click through to your eCommerce store to make a purchase.

Closer customers relationships

By connecting and interacting with your Social Media followers, you can build a closer relationship between your target audience and your business. This is done by interacting with them on your posts, replying to their questions and comments, and providing customer support.

Organic and Paid Social Media

In common with other publishing mediums (e.g. marketplaces, search), content can be published for free on Social Media platforms or users can pay to increase engagement. Content posted for free is referred to as Organic Social Media, whereas the content for which businesses pay to promote is called Paid Social Media.

Organic Social Media

This is the content (e.g. photos, posts or videos) users share freely on their profiles. When you post organically, the users who will see it are:

- A proportion of your followers (known as your 'organic reach').
- Your followers' followers (if your followers share your post).
- People following the hashtags you include.

However, because all the major platforms use ranking algorithms to organise the increasing amount of content, only a tiny proportion of your followers will see your organic posts. For example, the average organic reach for Facebook posts is just 5.5% of your follower count (Source: Hootsuite[125]) and this figure has been declining for several years.

In summary, if you rely on organic reach, it can be challenging to get your content in front of even a fraction of your existing followers, let alone any new followers.

Paid Social

Paid Social is when businesses pay social networks (e.g. Facebook, LinkedIn, Twitter or YouTube) to share their content with new audiences. This is either through 'boosting' their organic content or designing unique advertisements.

Businesses use Paid Social to:

- Raise brand awareness and attract new followers.
- Promote their latest deal, content or event.
- Generate leads.
- Drive conversions (including e-commerce sales).

Building your Social Media presence

Building up a Social Media following is challenging work. While there are 'Black Hat' techniques for quickly building followers, such as buying likes and followers, there are no shortcuts to creating a successful presence.

---

125   https://www.hootsuite.com/pages/digital-in-2019#accordion-148291

Strategies include:

Pick your platforms carefully

There is a bewildering array of social platforms, including Facebook, Instagram, Twitter, Snapchat, YouTube and Tumblr. It is easy to create accounts but much more challenging to maintain them. So, concentrate your efforts on a few select channels, as nothing looks worse than a neglected Social Media account.

Before launching an account, research the platforms where your target audience is most active. If you do not already know your customer profile, this information is available in Google Analytics and your current Social Media profiles. Demographic insights will include age, sex and location.

Craft your profiles

Social media accounts are highly ranked by Google and so will be one of the first things that potential customers see when they look for your business online. Consequently, you should create your profile carefully so it makes an excellent first impression:

- Choose a profile and cover image that is consistent with your brand.
- Complete all info sections, e.g. 'About Us.'
- Complete all contact information.
- Include relevant keywords for SEO.

Post frequently and respond to messages

The best way to build a Social Media following is to post quality content regularly and consistently. This might be once a week or several times every day. How often you post will depend on the nature of your business and your market. The key is consistency. You should also respond to customer messages and comments as this will build stronger connections and provide valuable feedback on your business.

The content you post will vary according to the platform, but typical content includes:

- Links to content on other channels (cross-posting). For example, you could post a link to a YouTube video on Twitter or Facebook.
- Blog posts
- Infographics
- Guest posts from influencers
- Relevant news links
- How-to guides
- Promotions and special offers
- New product launches

Whatever you post should be interesting, engaging content that encourages new customers to subscribe and old customers to stick around. If your messages are overly commercial (Buy! Buy! Buy!), this will be a turn off for customers. For best effect, mix up the content types above.

Engage with your followers

Your pages should be a welcoming space where people can spend time together, express their opinions and feel included. Consequently, you should always acknowledge people who respond to your content. Tag people in comments and like and reply to reviews and posts on your page – especially the negative ones.

Monitor performance

You should measure your Social Media performance and set targets. Social media metrics measure your posts' success and impact on your audience. They measure engagement, likes, follows, shares and other interactions on each platform.

Metrics include:

- **Engagement.** This includes clicks, likes, comments and replies to your Social Media posts. There are also platform-specific actions such as 'saved' Instagram posts and 'Pinned' Pinterest posts.
- **Reach.** Reach is the number of people who have seen your content.
- **Followers.** The number of people who opted to 'follow' your content and regularly see your content in their feeds.
- **Impressions.** The number of times a post is seen by users, e.g. when scrolling through their feed.
- **Video views.** The number of times a video you have posted is viewed.
- **Profile visits.** The number of users who have visited your page.
- **Mentions.** The number of times audience members have mentioned your profile in their posts.
- **Tags.** When a user adds the name of your company's profile or your hashtag to another post.
- **Reposts.** When a user posts your content on their profile.
- **Shares.** The posts your followers share with their network.

You should take advantage of the free analytics provided by most platforms. For example, posting the wrong content for your audience at an inappropriate time will hinder your posts' performance.

Valuable metrics to which you should pay attention include:

- Content that gets the best response, i.e. reactions, shares or comments.
- Days of the week and hours of the day when your followers are most active.
- Demographics of your audience: age, sex, location, interests.

There is, of course, no substitute for closely reading the activity on your Social Media profiles. Unfortunately, a post containing inappropriate content will still count as an engagement.

Consider Paid Social Media

If you want to build your followers quickly, consider promoting your posts to increase engagement.

Facebook

Facebook is world-dominating, with 68% of people in North America using the platform and 50% in Europe (source Statista[126]).

Since its launch, Facebook has become an integral part of peoples' online social presence. Though the level of engagement varies, for many people, Facebook is the only online social network they use. Facebook is built around connecting people, whether colleagues, friends, alumni or professional relationships.

Facebook Business Pages

Facebook Business Pages are a free opportunity for companies to increase brand awareness and generate sales via Facebook. Each page can be customised with a banner, logo, contact details and information about your business.

Once a page is created, the business can:

- Post content, e.g. text, photos, videos, links.
- Receive and reply to messages from customers.

---

126 https://www.statista.com/statistics/241552/share-of-global-population-using-facebook-by-region

- Open a Facebook shop (see below).
- Publish an action button to drive traffic to your website.
- Collect customer reviews or display reviews from third-party review services.
- Specify a vanity URL, e.g. facebook.com/yourbusinessname

Note: A Facebook business page is a requirement for using Facebook advertising.

WhatsApp and Facebook Messenger

Via a Facebook business page, customers can contact a business via Facebook messenger. These messages, alongside Instagram messages, will appear in the company's Facebook account. In addition, Facebook Messenger can be added to a website to power website live chat. The advantage of using Facebook Chat on a website is that most people already have a Facebook account, making it a reassuring experience.

Similarly, WhatsApp can be used for business communication, but it is not as easy to use as Facebook Messenger. However, Facebook is in the process of combining the two platforms.

Facebook/Instagram shops

Facebook business accounts can import a product feed to promote products across Facebook. For example, the products can be used in carousel ads or to populate a Facebook and Instagram storefront.

On the Facebook storefront, products are arranged into collections. Currently, if users click on a product, they will be redirected to an external product page. Whilst Facebook's eCommerce offering is limited, it is an area of focus for them and will undoubtedly develop into a marketplace-style offering.

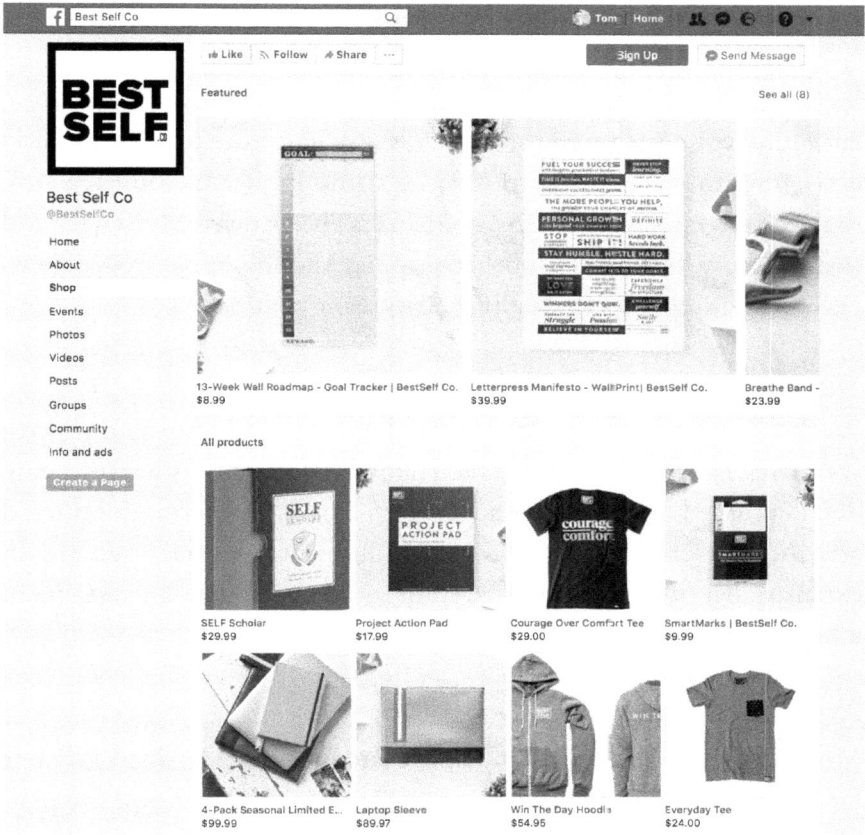

Fig. 39. Facebook storefront

Facebook Ads

One out of every ten advertising dollars is spent on Facebook advertising (Source HubSpot[127]). Its ability to enable businesses to reach customers based on their likes, interests and behaviours has made it a hugely successful and sometimes controversial advertising medium.

---

127 https://blog.hubspot.com/marketing/facebook-advertising-statistics

Facebook has the following advantages for advertisers:

Huge active user base

Facebook connects family and friends and has more than two billion active monthly users. As a result, we spend more time on Facebook than competing social networks. Also, Facebook owns Messenger and Instagram, which are two other popular mobile apps accessible to Facebook advertisers through its advertising platform.

Laser targeted

Facebook is built for sharing personal updates and information with your friends. All user actions taken on Facebook and Instagram create detailed user profiles which advertisers can access through targeted ads. Advertisers can match their products and services against an extensive list of users' interests, traits and behaviours. This results in a higher likelihood of reaching their ideal customers.

Generating brand awareness

Most businesses have a Facebook page and Instagram business account for connecting with their users on Social Media. When you use paid ads on Facebook and Instagram, you can opt to link them to your business page. This results in more brand exposure and new followers for your company.

Sophisticated advertising platform

Facebook has invested heavily into its advertising platform, resulting in a sophisticated and functionally rich suite of ad types and tools.

Types of Facebook Ads

Facebook Ads platform offers a wide range of ad types. Popular types of Facebook ads include:

- **Page likes.** Promote a Facebook Business Page to expand organic reach.

- **Post promotion.** Drive more engagement for organic posts to expand their original reach.
- **Images ads.** A simple image and description which drives traffic to an external website.
- **Video ads.** Like image ads but using a video instead of an image.
- **Carousel ads.** A carousel ad highlights a product or service by using up to 10 photos or videos.

Happy Socks
Sponsored
ID: 449596545900339

Look cooler than cool in bestselling Rubber Duck socks 🦆 HappySocks.com
Featuring your favorite bath-time buddy in shades, this cheerful design will have you smiling all day long.

 @dis.__.grace

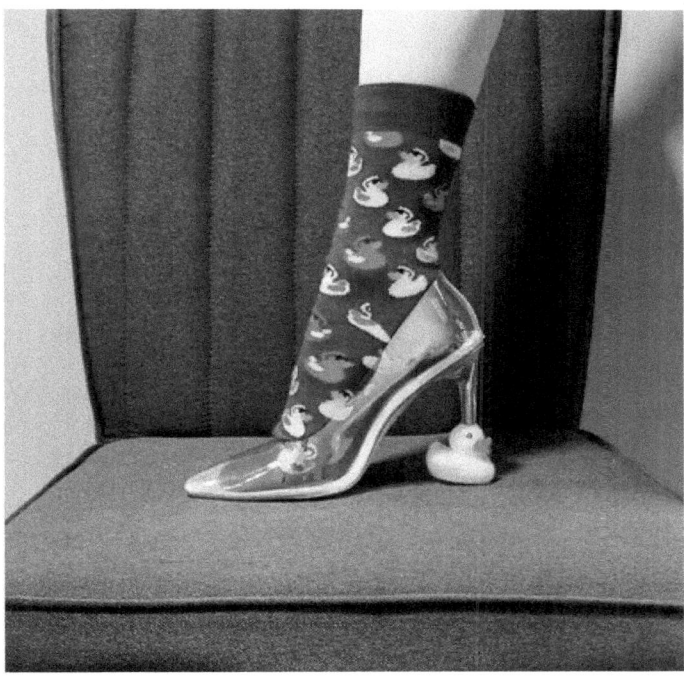

Bestseller: Rubber Duck Socks 🦆 😎
Don't miss out!   Shop Now
HAPPYSOCKS.COM

Fig. 40. Facebook image ad.

Creating a Facebook Ad campaign

To launch a campaign, you need to create a Facebook Business page. After that, you need to choose your objective, placements, specify a budget and choose a campaign type.

Choose your objective

On Facebook, advertisers can select from 11 marketing objectives based on what they want their ad to accomplish.

Here are how the objectives align with business goals:

- **Brand awareness.** Promote your brand to a new audience.
- **Reach.** Display your ad to people in your audience.
- **Traffic.** Drive traffic to a web page, app or Facebook Messenger conversation.
- **Engagement.** Reach a broad audience to increase the number of post engagements or Page Likes, promote an event or encourage people to claim an offer.
- **App installs.** Encourage app installs.
- **Video views.** Promote a video to get more views.
- **Lead generation.** Get sales prospects into your funnel.
- **Messages.** Encourage users to contact your company using Facebook Messenger.
- **Conversions.** Get people to take a specific action on your website (like subscribing to your newsletter or purchasing).
- **Catalogue sales.** Connect your Facebook ads to your product catalogue to show people ads for the products they want to buy.
- **Store traffic.** Drive nearby customers to local shops.

Each campaign can have a different objective. For example, you can pay-per-action for conversion-oriented goals (e.g. sales), but you will pay for impressions for exposure objectives (like traffic and views).

Choose placements

Facebook ads allow advertisers to specify where they wish their ads to appear. Initially, it is best to cast your net wide and then narrow your focus once ads have been running for a while. By then, you will know what works for you.

Options include:

- **Device type.** Mobile, desktop or both.
- **Platform.** Facebook, Instagram, WhatsApp or Messenger.
- **Placements.** Ad placements include news feeds, stories, in-stream (for videos), messages, in-article, apps and sites (external to Facebook).
- **Specific mobile devices and operating systems.** iOS, Android, feature phones or all devices.

Create a campaign and set a budget

When creating a Facebook campaign, it is necessary to select from the ad formats (see above) and define the creative shown to Facebook users.

- **Ad format.** Choose an ad format (see above).
- **Create advert.** Use the preview function to check that your ad looks ok in the placement you have chosen, e.g. mobile, tablet, desktop.
- **Schedule.** A campaign can run continuously or for a defined period.
- **Set budget.** Budget is specified daily.
- **Set bid.** Set the maximum bid for an action or 1000 impressions depending on the ad type.

Target your audience

When creating Facebook ads, the advertiser must specify an audience. The laser-like targeting that Facebook can offer its customers is one of the main reasons its ad platform is attractive to marketers. However, note that privacy legislation and Apple's iOS 15 restrictions may seriously compromise this in the future.

Facebook offers several options for creating audiences, either from your current customers or the broader Facebook userbase. As existing customers know and trust your brand, marketing to them can result in a significantly higher conversion rate.

Audience options include:

- **Customer lists.** Facebook allows advertisers to upload lists, e.g. newsletter subscribers or past customers. Note that you can only upload data from customers who have permitted you to market to them.
- **Website visitors.** By installing the Facebook pixel on the page of your site, Facebook can match your website visitors to their Facebook profiles.
- **Custom Audiences.** These audiences allow you to target people who have already interacted with your brand on Facebook or Instagram.
- **Lookalike audiences.** If you do not have enough customers to whom you can advertise, you can increase your reach by specifying a lookalike audience. These are Facebook users that resemble your custom audience.

All campaigns must specify a target location, age, gender and language. There is also the option to select details targeting options for demographics, interests and behaviours.

Facebook tracking: the Facebook Pixel

The Facebook 'pixel' is code you place on your website. It works by dropping cookies that track users interacting with your website and your Facebook ads across multiple devices. This helps track conversions from Facebook ads, optimise ads, build targeted audiences for future ads and remarket to users who have already interacted with your website.

The Facebook pixel allows advertisers to do the following:

- Track interaction with your website after viewing your Facebook ad.
- Display targeted ads to users who have already been to your site. (known as retargeting).
- Build lookalike audiences of users who have similar likes, interests and demographics to users already interacting with your website.
- Optimise your Facebook ads for specific conversion events on your website.

Even if you are not yet advertising on Facebook, installing the pixel is a good idea. This is because installing the pixel will enable Facebook to collect data right away. This will make any future Facebook ad campaigns more successful as they have more data from which to predict customer behaviour data.

Instagram

Instagram is a visual Social Media platform that enables photo and video sharing via its mobile app. Users can take, edit and publish visual content with which their followers can interact through likes, comments and shares.

With over a billion users, Instagram, bought by Facebook in 2012, has become a part of daily life. Over the last few years, this simple photo-sharing application evolved into a massive marketing and retail platform used by over 25 million companies.

Instagram content types

Unlike Facebook or Twitter, which rely on both text and pictures, Instagram's primary purpose is to empower users to share images or videos with their audience.

Like other platforms, users post content and follow other users. Following other users means that their posts appear in your feed. Users can see the people you are following and who is following you. In addition, users can comment on each other's posts and messages.

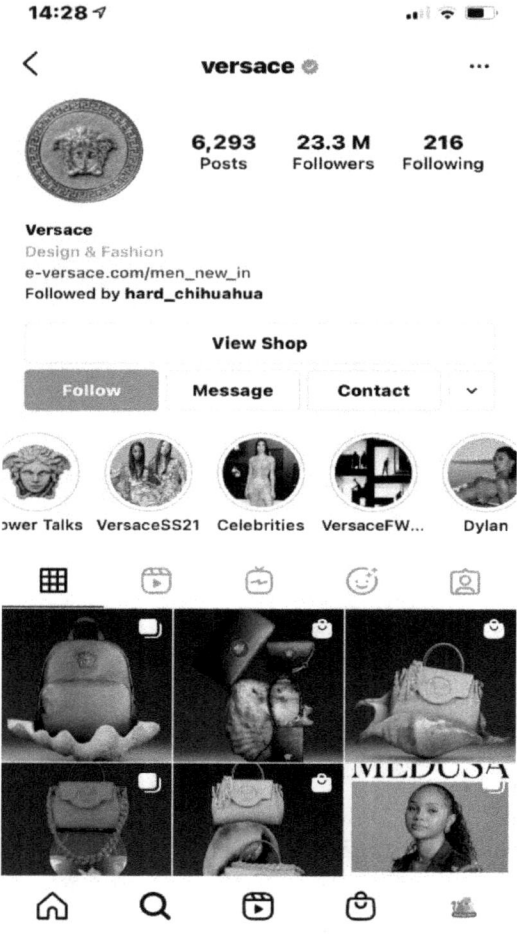

Fig. 41. Instagram profile

Posts

These are the photos and videos with a caption, which you upload to share with your followers. Followers can interact with your content by liking, commenting, saving and sharing your post.

Stories

Stories appear in a separate feed at the top of your profile page. They expire after one day and are often more casually used than posts. They are frequently used to expand on something featured in a post.

IGTV

Instagram TV (IGTV) is Instagram's dedicated video platform that lets users post videos up to 15 minutes long (60 minutes on the desktop version). IGTV has a dedicated app for iPhone and Android, but you can also find it within the regular Instagram app.

Reels

Inspired by TikTok, Instagram Reels are short-form videos. They have a separate feed on the profile.

Instagram business accounts

An Instagram business account has all the features of an Instagram personal account but with the following additional benefits:

- **Instagram ads.** These are managed through the Facebook ads interface.
- **Insights.** Information on your followers, including gender, location and reach.
- **Instagram shop.** A shopfront populated by items tagged in photos.
- **Company info.** Contact info and call to action.

Instagram shop

Users can shop for your items directly on Instagram if you sell physical products. If you have set up an Instagram shop from within your business account, products can be tagged in posts and these will then appear in the Instagram shop. Like the Facebook shop, clicking on a product will take the user to the account holder's website.

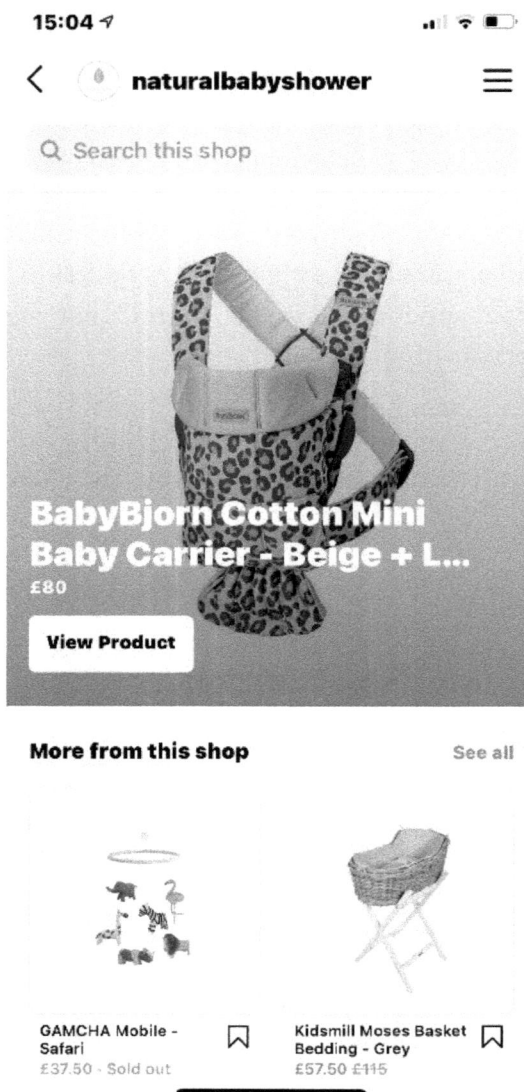

Fig. 42. Instagram shop

Instagram Ads

With an audience of more than a billion people, Instagram offers extraordinary reach for brands. 60% of users say they discover new products on the platform and 75% of users act after seeing an inspiring post (Source: Instagram[128]).

The platform has a young demographic, with the most significant percentage of users falling in the age range of 18-29 (55%), then between 30 and 49 years old (28%). Only 11% of users are 50-64 and just 4% are over 65.

Instagram advertising is accessed through the Facebook ads platform and offers the same targeting options as Facebook ads. As Instagram is a visual platform, ads also take the form of pictures or videos.

Twitter

Twitter is a 'microblogging' platform that allows users to send and receive short posts called tweets. Tweets are up to 280 characters long and include links to relevant websites and images. Twitter users follow other users and if you follow someone, you can see their tweets in your Twitter 'timeline'. You can follow people, companies or other organisations with similar interests to you.

With more than 145 million active daily users (Source: Hootsuite[129]), Twitter is one of the most popular Social Media networks. Twitter has the potential to be a great promotional tool for your company and products. It provides an excellent channel for connecting with your target audience and bringing them the tailored content that will help convert them into customers.

128　https://business.instagram.com/getting-started

129　https://blog.hootsuite.com/twitter-statistics

Twitter terminology

Retweets

Retweeting someone else's tweet on your Twitter feed is similar to a like on Facebook. Retweeting allows information to be shared quickly and efficiently with many people.

Fig. 43. Example tweet with image and link. This tweet has been retweeted 22 times and liked 322 times.

Hashtags

Adding a "#" to the beginning of an unbroken word (or combination of words) creates a hashtag on Twitter. When a hashtag is used in a Tweet, the Tweet becomes linked to all the other Tweets that include it. Including a hashtag gives a Tweet context. Tweets that include hashtags get almost double the engagement of Tweets without hashtags.

For example, the tweets below all include the hashtag #brexit.

Selvaseelan Selvarajah @DrSelvarajah · Feb 14   ···
The same people who told us #Brexit would be amazingly beneficial to 🇬🇧 are telling us having absolutely no safeguards in the middle of the pandemic is a good idea.

♡ 43   ⟲ 526   ♡ 2,230   ↥

Loz Argyle ⚓ @ArgyleLoz · Feb 10   ···
Without a doubt John Major is the only Conservative with any backbone, he rightly calls out the #Brexit lies, the English Nationa ism that Johnson has invoked, he speaks so much sense, unlike his cowardly colleagues he can see the damage Johnson is doing to our democracy...

♡ 28   ⟲ 216   ♡ 1,046   ↥

Jon Danzig #FBPE @Jon_Danzig · Feb 14   ···
Blame politicians, not voters, for #Brexit. We can't win without voters. RT this 2-minute clip of @mrjamesob on @LBC who said, "Blame the people who sold Brexit, not the people who bought it." My full report on Facebook: bit.ly/3gMSPcc LinkedIn: bit.ly/3oNb5H5

Fig.44. Tweets using the #Brexit

Mentions

When someone includes your Twitter username (a.k.a. your handle, e.g. @hellobabydirect), they are either talking to you or about you in a tweet. Twitter is where customers contact brands, especially if they are unhappy, so it is essential to monitor tweets that include your handle.

Should my business be on Twitter?

Around 76% of Twitter users already follow brands and about one-third of these are retailers. Retailers underuse Twitter to the extent that many users would like more content from the brands they follow. For example, 25% would like to see more offers. 46% of the retail audience have linked to a brand on Twitter and, after viewing retail related tweets, 45% have engaged in further research. (Source: Twitter[130])

Amazon.co.uk ✓
@AmazonUK

Spring offers are now here with Amazon's Early Easter Sale!

1:04 PM · Mar 19, 2018

♡ 52   ♡ 44   ⬆ Share this Tweet

Fig. 45. Example of a tweet used to promote an offer

---

130 https://blog.twitter.com/en_gb/topics/marketing/2018/twitter-retail-research.html

Twitter Ads

Using paid ads on Twitter is a fantastic way to reach your audience more directly rather than waiting for users to discover your profile organically. They allow people to find your profile, even if they do not follow your brand or hashtags. When you promote a Tweet, it shows up in the timelines of users who share interests with your followers. Users interact with promoted Tweets in the same way as organic content.

Pinterest

Pinterest is a visual discovery network that can be used to find ideas for projects and interests. It is a way to collect and virtually categorise things you like.

Pinners come to the platform for inspiration or 'Pinspiration.' They are planning their weddings, interior decoration or holidays. Because of this, they are not only receptive to brand content -they find it helpful.

Should my business be on Pinterest?

Eighty-four per cent of users use Pinterest to help decide what to buy. According to Pinterest, 55% of Pinners are explicitly searching for products and 83% of users have made a purchase based on the content they see from brands on Pinterest (Source: Pinterest[131])

Pinners like to discover new products. Compared with 55% on other digital channels, 75% of Pinterest users say they are interested in new products. In addition, 77% per cent of users regularly discover brands and products on Pinterest. (Source: Pinterest[132])

---

131 https://business.pinterest.com/en-gb/insights/the-point
132 Ibid

- 300 million global monthly active users.
- 83% of weekly users have bought based on the content they saw from brands on Pinterest.
- Pinners spend 80% more on shopping than non-pinners

(Source: Pinterest[133])

How Pinterest works

Every idea is represented by a Pin on Pinterest, an image that Pinterest users can search and save. Pins can also link back to websites, so Pinterest is excellent for driving traffic and sales.

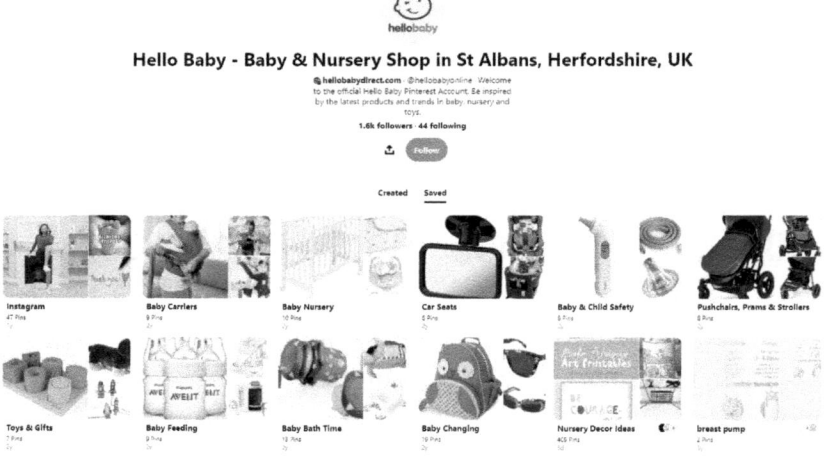

Fig. 46. Pinterest storefront.

RePins

A RePin is when a user pins something they did not create to one of their boards.

---

133   Ibid

Rich Pins

Rich Pins provide more information on a pin, including price and install buttons. They are available in four formats: Product, Recipe, Article and App Pins.

Boards and group boards

Pinterest boards are a digital version of mood boards. They are used to group pins together around a particular theme or topic. For example, you might create a board for a product launch or seasonal content. Group boards are similar, except more than one person can add content.

Pinterest business profiles and shops

Pinterest offers a business account with several tools to help businesses make the most of the platform.

- **Analytics.** Metrics on the performance of your pins and ads.
- **Shop.** Merchants can submit a feed of their live products, which automatically creates pins. These pins will appear under the account's shop tab.
- **Ads.** Pinterest ads enable companies to promote their Pins or product catalogue and drive traffic to their site.

Pinterest Ads

Pinterest offers a sophisticated advertising platform that enables the advertising of promoted pins to users based on their interests and demographics. Promoted pins can either be Pins made by the account or products uploaded from a feed.

Promoted Pins

Promoted pins are regular pins that businesses have paid to promote. Promoted pins appear in home feeds and search results and include the 'Promoted' label. Other options include promoted video pins, carousel and app pins.

Catalogue sales

Pinterest Shopping ads help engage with customers as they seek inspiration. Pinterest uses your product data to show relevant products to interested people. Two formats of shop ads are available:

- **Shopping ads.** Ads show a single product.
- **Collections ad.** A group of products is shown as a single ad.

YouTube

YouTube is a free video sharing site where over two billion users watch a billion hours of videos every day. The site is the second most popular site online (after Google.com) and the second largest search engine (Source: YouTube[134]).

Despite its massive popularity, only 9% of small businesses have a YouTube Channel (Source: Brandwatch[135]), so it is far from a saturated channel.

YouTube Channels

A channel is a member's presence on YouTube where other users can view all their videos. Users customise their channel by creating a branded header, adding an intro video and organising their videos into playlists.

---

134   https://www.searchenginejournal.com/seo-101/meet-search-engines
135   https://www.brandwatch.com/blog/youtube-stats

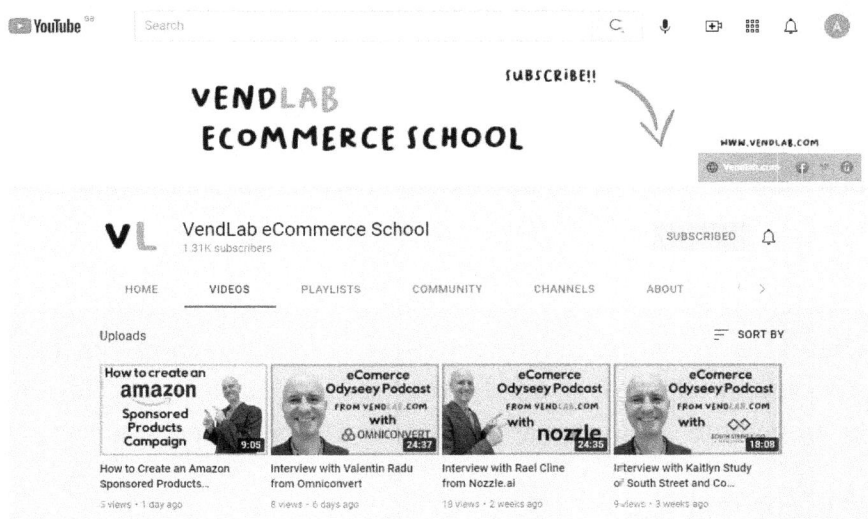

Fig. 47. Youtube channel homepage

What to post

Video should be an important part of your content marketing strategy. It is a fantastic way to provide your customers with high-quality, informative and entertaining content which keeps them coming back repeatedly. Furthermore, as YouTube is the second-largest search engine globally, optimising your videos for search can also be a wonderful place to connect with new customers.

Videos should be engaging for your audience. You want to create exciting content which will naturally pick up views. Good engagement metrics will improve a video's search rankings (see below).

Educational content

Increasingly, people are turning to YouTube to learn new things. Searches for instructional videos have grown 140% over the past 13 years. Businesses can find new customers by publishing educational content related to their products. Educational videos are great for building trust with your audience and nudging them further down the conversion funnel.

Brand stories

Inspirational videos that fit your company's identity are perfect for communicating your brand's image and ideals to a broader audience. In addition, aspirational videos can build a lifestyle around your brand and show customers that, when they purchase your products, they are not just buying something, they are buying an experience.

Entertainment

One of the most effective ways to capture viewers' attention, and focus it on your products, is to build a YouTube content strategy. This can be around fun videos that appeal to your audience's interests.

YouTube metrics

Once your YouTube channel has launched, you should track its performance. Here are the most important metrics available in YouTube Analytics:

- **Watch Time.** Amount of time spent watching your content.
- **Traffic source.** This shows how people find your videos by displaying the traffic sources and the views per source.
- **Subscriber rate.** How subscriber numbers change on a video-by-video basis.
- **Audience retention.** This shows the exact times when people stop watching your video. You can use this information to determine where you lost a viewer's attention and what may have caused them to leave.

Firstly, decide the goals for your YouTube channel, as this will help you determine which metrics are the most important for your business. For example, if you want to know how your audience engages with your content, you can monitor watch time and see how many viewers convert into subscribers.

Promoting your YouTube channel

Optimising videos for search

Staying on top of your YouTube SEO (Search Engine Optimisation) is critical if you want to get your videos seen. Five hundred hours of video are added to YouTube every minute, so you need to work hard to stand out from the crowd.

Many different elements of your videos can impact how prominently they are featured in search results. Ensure that you research the best keywords for each video and include these in your video description. A reliable source of keywords is YouTube search autocomplete.

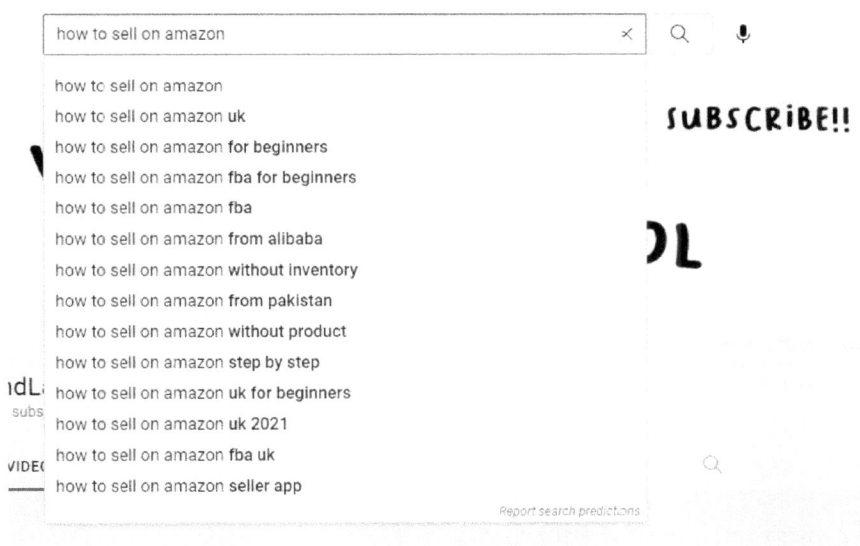

Fig. 48. YouTube search autocomplete

The areas of a video to optimise include:

Title

Your video's title should be concise, descriptive and feature your target keyword near the start.

Filename

Include target keywords in the uploaded file's name as this is a factor that YouTube considers.

Length

The YouTube algorithm considers longer videos to be of higher value so try to make substantial videos. However, always balance this with keeping the content interesting as watch time is another critical metric for search rankings.

Description

The description should give a detailed overview of your video and link to relevant resources. Use keywords in the description, particularly in the first sentence.

Tags

Include your target keywords and relevant terms as tags on your videos. Tags also help determine whether your video shows up as a suggested video. In addition, tagging competitors and channels making related content can effectively use the 500 characters available for tags.

Cross-promotion

Promote videos on other social networks like Instagram (through posts and Instagram Stories), Facebook or TikTok. Another option is to partner with other YouTubers to increase your content's reach.

Engage with your subscribers

To make a YouTube channel successful, you should interact with your viewers to create conversations on your videos and get more YouTube subscribers.

You should respond to viewers comments (including negative ones), ask and answer questions and like comments. Users can then see which comments are the most important to read. Another option is to poll your audience to see what content they want to watch.

Advertising your channel

It takes time to promote your YouTube channel organically. So you can invest in YouTube ads to reach and engage with more viewers to speed things up. YouTube ads are managed through the Google Ads platform. See Chapter 5 for more details.

Blogging

If your business website does not have a blog (short for weblog), you miss a significant opportunity to engage with your customers and increase website traffic. A static website that does not change, or feature updated content, is an online brochure that will not chime well with users. In addition, Google search awards higher placement to sites featuring new content.

A blog consists of a chronological list of articles or 'posts' in the online journal format. Blogs have a unique terminology. A *blogger* writes a blog and the act of writing a blog is *blogging*.

Blogs all have the following features in common:

- **Chronological order.** The front page of a blog consists of a list of the latest posts in date order. Older posts are pushed off the front page as new posts are added.
- **Simple to use.** Blogs are typically managed by a simple content management system such as WordPress and Blogger. This allows them to be created and edited with little technical knowledge.
- **Comments.** Readers can add comments to each blog post. Comments are critical in blogs as they change the post from a simple article into a conversation.
- **Archives.** Older posts are archived by theme.

Blogging for business

Blogs can be a powerful tool for businesses, allowing them to promote their brand and form closer bonds with their customers.

What makes a good (business) blog?

A good blog will be frequently updated with exciting entries which showcase the blogger's knowledge and passion for a particular subject. Companies should not just broadcast commercial messages as these will not make for an interesting blog and may be off-putting to customers.

Successful bloggers engage in their communities by responding to comments and commenting on other blogs. Blog posts should also reference other blogs, providing pointers for further research. A business blog will be more interesting if it includes a representative sample of the company employees. It should consist of news and views from people throughout the organisation, giving a complete and balanced idea of working there.

A company blog will not be effective if used to publish press releases and impersonal corporate news. Instead, a blog should show the more human face of the company while giving customers and other stakeholders an insight into the company's workings, its products and the people who make it tick.

Things to blog about

Here is a selection of simple ideas for writing an excellent corporate blog.

- **How-to guides.** Write simple guides that enable your customer to get more out of your products. Emphasize the importance of the aspects of your product that set it apart from the competition.
- **New products.** Offering promotions to your blog's readers is a great way to launch new products.

- **Employee profiles.** To give people more insight into your company, get a diverse range of company workers to write about their experiences.
- **Job opportunities.**

Benefits of business blogging

Brand-building and demonstrating expertise

A well-positioned blog can help build a company's brand and reputation. By writing posts related to their products and industry, such as guides or case studies, a business demonstrates knowledge of its field and differentiates itself from the competition. A blog can also help personalise a company, giving the organisation a more human face.

Search Engine Marketing

Blogs are one of the most effective tools for search engine optimisation. This is because blogs have many features which make them attractive to search engine algorithms.

- **Frequent updates.** Search engines are known to promote sites that have frequently updated content.
- **Quality content.** Enjoyable content attracts readers and provides the text for search engines to index.
- **Link building.** Blogs can quickly attract quality incoming links due to the blogging community's highly interlinked nature. Links are a vital search engine ranking factor.
- **Search engine friendly.** The most popular blog platforms are search-engine friendly, allowing easy spidering.

Besides attracting search engine visitors, a good blog will be 'sticky' by its very nature. Quality content naturally encourages people to revisit. Features such as notifying users about comments can also bring return visitors. Quality content is also more likely to be shared.

News distribution

All companies have news to distribute, including press releases or informal announcements. Blogs provide a suitable medium for publishing company activities. In addition, syndication through Social Media allows posts to be easily distributed.

The ease of publishing means that news is no longer a big event but is a constant stream of information. It allows an organisation to be more transparent to its customers. A company blog will not be effective if it simply publishes staid press releases and impersonal corporate news. Instead, a blog should show a more human face of the company, giving customers and other stakeholders an insight into the company's workings, its products and the people who make it tick.

How to get your blog read

There is not much point in writing a blog if nobody will read it. Unfortunately, there are no shortcuts to creating a successful blog. Promoting a blog takes time and hard work.

Content is king

A professionally written, informative and frequently updated blog will naturally encourage visitors to subscribe so they can return and follow your content on Social Media. In addition, as covered in the SEO chapter, enjoyable content will also attract incoming links and provide additional text to be indexed and searched by the major search engines.

Guest-posting

One way to create engaging content is to invite other bloggers and industry experts to contribute. This benefits both parties as the contributor gains extra publicity and your blog obtains kudos from associating with an industry expert. To gain new readers for your blog, consider contributing to other blogs as a guest blogger.

SEO your blog

A blog is a website that improves its natural search engine performance by carefully employing the search engine optimisation techniques covered in Chapter 4.

Cross-posting on Social Media

Sharing your blog post on your Social Media accounts is one of the best ways to promote your content. Writing a blog makes content that can create compelling Social Media posts. These will drive traffic to your site.

To structure your posting create a Social Media content calendar based on holidays and seasons.

Summary

Almost all your customers and potential customers are on Social Media. They expect companies to have a presence on the major Social Media networks (Facebook, Twitter, Instagram) and often prefer to use their Social Media accounts to send customer service queries. Therefore, if your company does not have a strong presence on the major networks, you will lose out to more active competitors.

Regular posting is a wonderful way to form closer bonds with your customers and is a free way to build your brand, drive traffic and generate sales. Create helpful content for your target audience and limit overtly commercial messages. With the enormous volume of content published every day, frequently the only way to get your content read is by paying to promote it (a.k.a. boosting content).

The major Social Media Networks have advertising platforms designed to help build businesses a following and acquire customers.

The amount of data these platforms hold on their users means that ads can be laser targeted to a specific demographic.

Resources

A comprehensive list of Social Media platforms can be found on that font of all knowledge, Wikipedia:

https://en.wikipedia.org/wiki/List_of_social_networking_services

If you are researching which Social Media platform is most relevant to your audience, Sprout Social has put together a list of Social Media demographic data:

https://sproutsocial.com/insights/new-social-media-demographics/

If you are wondering what the demographics of your customers are, this can be obtained from Google Analytics or from within your current Social Media platforms.

PART III:

INCREASING SALES THROUGH ONLINE MARKETPLACES

M arketplaces like eBay and Amazon are great places to do business because they have millions of loyal customers and an international reach. Set up costs are low and by publishing your inventory on these marketplaces, you will quickly get incremental sales. On the downside, they can be a hassle and their rules are heavily biased towards the buyer.

Pros and cons of online marketplaces

If you are not selling on marketplaces, you are missing out on 40% of the eCommerce market. Marketplaces are easy to use and low-hanging fruit for any online retailer. You may not like them, but they are where your customers want to shop much of the time. Their benefits are legion:

- **Easy to use.** Listing products on marketplaces is straightforward, requiring no technical skills.
- **One-stop-shop.** Marketplaces provide a platform for publishing products, a search engine for finding products and checkout to complete the sale. Because of this, many businesses do not bother with a website.
- **Low up-front costs.** The setup cost and ongoing subscription fees are low. For example, an Amazon professional account is £30/month.
- **Success fee.** Most marketplace fees are commission-based, i.e. payment made for completed sales.
- **Enormous customer base.** Amazon alone has over 300 million users worldwide and a 49% share of the US eCommerce market.

- **International scope.** Marketplaces are a terrific way to connect with customers all over the world. For example, both Amazon and eBay have a presence in around 20 countries.
- **Safe.** Marketplaces intermediate between buyers and sellers, providing a safe place for business.

On the other hand, when you sell on marketplaces, you must abide by their rules and pay their fees. Whilst not usually too much of an issue, it can be frustrating.

- **Expensive.** Commission fees range from around 10% to 15%.
- **Do not own customer.** Customers belong to the marketplace. Trying to market to them can get your account suspended. You do not have their direct email addresses and cannot encourage them to make future purchases.
- **Strict rules.** It is all too easy to fall afoul of marketplace rules. For example, diverting customers to your website can get your account suspended.
- **Customer-focused.** Marketplaces focus on the interests of the customer over the seller.

Despite their enormous success, many brands look down on marketplaces (especially eBay), feeling that associating with online marketplaces cheapens their brand. However, while allowing products to be sold on marketplaces means that a brand will lose some control over pricing and presentation, customers are loyal to marketplaces and may switch to other brands if their first choice is unavailable.

9:

AMAZON

Amazon has come a long way since its inception as an online bookseller. The site is now the number one eCommerce site in the West and sells in 14 categories, including books, electronics, home and garden, sports and baby. Worldwide, Amazon has 300 million customers with sales of £300 billion.

As well as being a leading online retailer, Amazon allows other retailers to sell products through their platform. Amazon calls this service the Amazon marketplace and there are now 5 million third-party sellers on Amazon. Offers from third-party sellers are presented alongside Amazon's offers, giving buyers a range of purchasing options.

I have mixed feelings about Amazon. I would not have a business without it, as Amazon sales total about 30% of my business in the UK and internationally. However, selling on Amazon requires dancing to Amazon's tune and every year they seem to add more and more hoops through which retailers must jump.

There is no denying that people love Amazon! Retailers must be where their customers are so you ignore it at your peril.

Pros and cons of selling through Amazon

Benefits

Selling through Amazon provides businesses with an additional, potentially high-volume channel to sell stock and should be considered part of the eCommerce strategy of every eCommerce business.

Ease of use

By selling through Amazon, small businesses can avoid the trouble of setting up a website and attracting customers. Amazon provides a one-stop-shop for selling online.

Enormous international marketplace

You benefit from Amazon's massive customer base by selling on the Amazon marketplace. Amazon has an online retailing presence in 19 countries and £300 billion in sales worldwide. Places like Japan are difficult to reach in any other way.

Secure payment system and limited fraud

All payments through the Amazon marketplace are guaranteed, protecting you from credit card chargebacks or online fraud.

Free listing

Amazon does not charge a listing fee, only a commission when an item sells. Consequently, selling on Amazon is risk-free, allowing you to list your entire inventory.

Drawbacks

Selling on Amazon can be an undignified experience. Fees are high and the highly automated nature of their business can make you feel like a very tiny cog in a vast machine.

High fees

Amazon's final value fees vary by category but are typically 15% of the item's sale value for professional sellers.

Lack of customisation

The Amazon system allows minimal customisation to the extent that buyers will frequently buy from a marketplace seller but think they are purchasing from Amazon.

You do not own the customer

Amazon does not allow sellers to market to buyers and all communication is through a cloaked email address. It is against Amazon's rules to market to Amazon customers and you can get suspended for this.

Time-consuming

Both Amazon and their customers are demanding and the number of metrics you must adhere to grows year on year. Amazon always focuses on the customer at your expense. For example:

- **Time-consuming.** Managing feedback and claims is laborious.
- **Customer Biased.** The customer almost always wins A-Z claims. (See below)
- **High return rates.** Amazon makes returning items easy and obligates sellers to offer free returns.
- **Oppressive metrics.** Amazon is forever raising the performance levels required of sellers, adding new metrics to be monitored and managed.

Lack of control

Amazon is a vast, faceless corporation. It can and does suspend accounts. If your business depends too much on Amazon, this can be disastrous.

The Amazon Marketplace

Amazon is a catalogue-based marketplace. To sell an item already for sale on Amazon, you can simply add your offer (the price and condition) to a product listing without the need to specify any other details such as description or photographs. This makes it easy for businesses to get started.

All sales, including those from third-party sellers, are paid for through the same Amazon checkout and a buyer can pay for products from multiple sellers all at the same time. All payments must go through Amazon with no direct contact between buyer and seller.

The simplicity of the marketplace has enabled third-party sellers to list substantial amounts of inventory on Amazon, expanding Amazon's catalogue and offering more choices to consumers. In large part, due to its marketplace, Amazon has experienced stellar growth of its core business.

Tip: Amazon marketplace is based around barcodes, with each product listing being for a single barcoded product. If you have a list of barcodes for your products, these can be used to match against the Amazon catalogue, creating your product inventory at lightning speed!

Amazon Marketplace seller levels

The Amazon marketplace is available to all Amazon members but Amazon has different subscription levels for individuals and business customers.

Basic account

This is the free, entry-level seller subscription on Amazon. Basic account holders cannot create listings, only add their offer to existing listings. They also pay a fixed fee on each sale along with the commission.

Professional account

For volume sellers, the Professional Seller tier has the following benefits:

- **Discounted fees.** Professional sellers do not pay a per-item fee.
- **Buy Box eligibility.** Only Professional sellers have access to the Buy Box (see Featured Offer below).
- **Create inventory items in bulk.** Professional sellers can add products to the Amazon catalogue in bulk.
- **Set postage.** Professional sellers can define postage rates for their offers based on either item weight or cost.
- **More categories.** Some categories can only be accessed by professional sellers.

Tip: Unless you are a hobby seller with meagre sales, you should sign up for a professional level Amazon seller account.

Payments

All payments between buyer and seller go via Amazon. By being a central counterparty to all marketplace transactions, Amazon protects buyers and sellers against fraud and chargebacks and offers a pain-free way to purchase products. Amazon pays sellers (minus Amazon fees) on a 14-day cycle.

Fees

While not charging an upfront listing fee, Amazon takes a hefty percentage of the item's sale price. Professional Amazon sellers pay a fee of 15% (with a lower rate for some categories) of the product's sale price + postage.

Amazon feedback

Amazon buyers can leave feedback for sellers, but only about 5-10% do. Feedback is on a scale of 1 to 5 with 1 or 2 a negative, 3 neutral and 4 or 5 a positive. Feedback is used to measure seller performance and feeds into Buy Box performance.

Tip: As a negative feedback rate of greater than 1% puts the account in danger of suspension, it pays to keep on top of it. You can request the removal of reviews about the product and not the service.

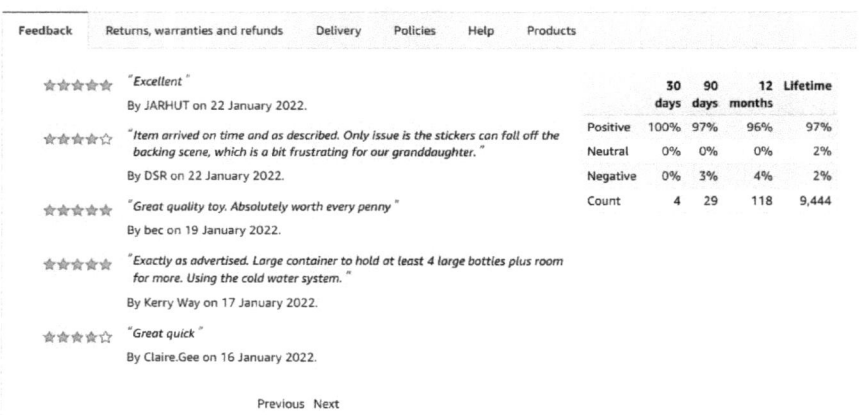

Fig. 49. Amazon seller's feedback profile

Amazon A-Z Guarantee

The A-Z guarantee scheme is Amazon's guarantee to customers that they will receive the products they purchased through the marketplace or get their money back. It covers the following situations:

- Non-delivery of orders.
- Delivered products were different from the Amazon listing.

Under these situations, buyers initiate a claim against the seller, which Amazon mediates. A seller can end the procedure by refunding the customer or if they feel that the customer is mistaken, they can make their case to Amazon.

The percentage of A-Z claims counts toward a seller's Order Defect rate (see below). Too many A-Z claims can get an account suspended.

Tip: In my experience, Amazon rarely favours marketplace sellers, so once an A-Z claim has been raised, it is best to end it quickly.

Amazon Prime

Amazon Prime is a subscription service where members qualify for free shipping on their Amazon purchases and other benefits, e.g. Prime video and music for a fixed annual fee. This product has driven sales across the Amazon platform, including Marketplace sales. Amazon Prime subscribers are loyal Amazon customers who make frequent purchases. Marketplace products benefit from being 'Prime eligible' when shipped by Fulfilled by Amazon (FBA) or Seller Fulfilled Prime.

Being Prime eligible is a crucial driver of sales on Amazon so maximise the number of your listings that are 'Prime Eligible', either by fulfilling them via Seller Fulfilled Prime or FBA. There are over 200 million Prime members in 22 countries and, by ensuring your offers are Prime eligible, you can reach this high spending group of customers. Prime members are Amazon's most loyal customers and place an average of 24 orders a year (value $1,400), whereas non-Prime customers only place 13[136] (value $600[137]). In addition, Prime customers value free, speedy delivery and frequently filter to see only Prime eligible offers.

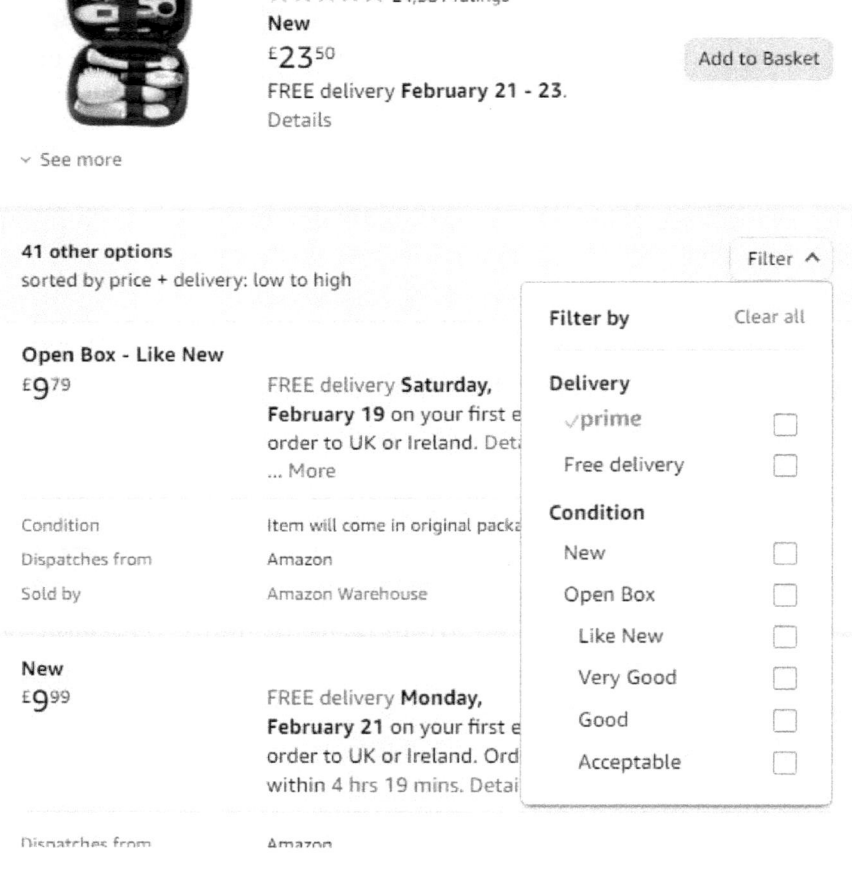

Fig. 50. Prime filtering on Amazon product listing

136   https://www.statista.com/topics/4076/amazon-prime

137   https://www.statista.com/statistics/304938/amazon-prime-and-non-prime-members-average-sales-spend

Amazon listings

Each product in the Amazon catalogue has a single listing on the website, known as a product detail page. The product detail page will display information about the product and give several buying options.

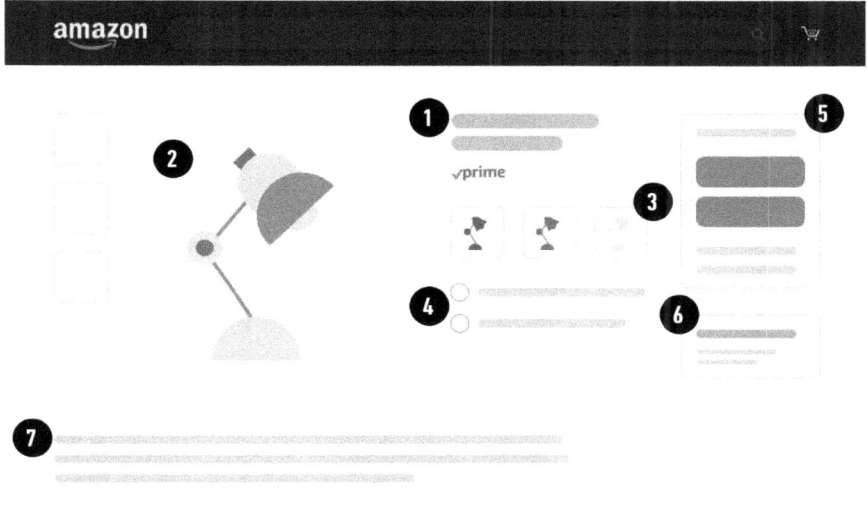

Fig. 51. Part of the Amazon product detail page.

1. **Title.** The product title is a maximum of 200 characters and you should aim for at least 80 characters. Include your top 5 keywords and capitalise each word.

2. **Images.** Aim for at least five high-quality images (min 1000 pixels on the longest side). The product should be on a white background for the primary photo and be 85% of the picture.

3. **Variations.** Such as colours, quantity or sizes.

4. **Bullet points.** Up to 5 points that highlight key features and benefits.

5. **Featured offer.** ('Buy Box') The featured offer on a detail page. Customers can add to their cart or 'Buy Now.'

6. **Other offers.** The same product sold by other sellers offering different prices and shipping options.
7. **Description.** Write a description that gives clear and precise information about the product. Can use HTML to structure.

Not shown on the diagram

- **Reviews.** Customer reviews of your products.
- **Questions and Answers.** Customer questions.
- **A+ Content.** A rich-content section available to brands and used to give more information about the product. Amazon says using this feature increases conversion.
- **Additional product information.** Further information about each product, such as material, weight or energy-efficiency class.

Featured offer

Many Amazon listings will have offers from multiple sellers. Of these, one will appear as the featured offer in the 'Buy Box.' This is the default offer for buyers and will receive the lion's share of orders. Other buying options are displayed on the product detail page under the Buy Box as 'more buying options.' Clicking on more buying options will link to an ordered list of offers.

This system rewards sellers who offer good customer service and competitive prices. Every Amazon seller aims to get their offer into the Buy Box. Winning the Buy Box is crucial, as 80-90% of Amazon sales go to the offer in the Buy Box.

Amazon rotates the featured offer for listings with multiple sellers, giving high placement to sellers who perform well in the following areas:

Price

The 'landed price' (item plus shipping) is one of the most influential factors when Amazon awards the Buy Box. Being cheaper by £0.01 can be enough to win over another offer.

Prime eligibility and fulfilment method

Amazon takes the fulfilment method's quality very seriously and offers fulfilled by Amazon (FBA) or Seller Fulfilled Prime (SFP) have a better chance of being the Featured Offer. Also, Prime members will often filter out non-prime offers entirely. For more information on FBA and SFP, see the section on fulfilment options below.

Availability

Amazon will give a higher ranking to offers that have better availability. For example, offer A, which is available in 1-2 days, will rank higher than offer B, which is available in 1-2 weeks, even if offer A is more expensive than product B.

Performance metrics

Your performance metrics also influence box performance. All other things being equal, sellers with better performance metrics will rank higher. The most crucial metric is Order Defect Rate (ODR).

The ODR is the percentage of sales that were not perfect, i.e. an order which receives one of:

- **Negative feedback.** Orders which received negative feedback (defined as a score of 1 or 2 out of 5). Neutral feedback (3 out of 5) does not count against the seller.
- **Credit card chargeback.** Amazon treats a chargeback like a piece of negative feedback.
- **A-Z guarantee claim.** A-Z claims are complaints by customers that a product did not arrive or was not as advertised.

Each order will only count once toward the ODR. Other important metrics include refund rate and late shipment rate.

Dynamic pricing

With price being a significant factor in determining which offer gets placed into the Buy Box, it is vital to monitor price carefully and adjust pricing to remain competitive. However, if you are selling many products, it becomes impractical to price manually and it is best to use one of the many 'repricers' available to manage pricing.

Typically, these tools work in the following way:

- **Select products.** Import details of the products whose price you wish to manage.
- **Select competition.** Set the parameters of the products against which you wish to reprice. For example, you may only want to compare prices against products with the same fulfilment method or delivery timescale or sellers above a specific feedback score.
- **Set pricing.** The tool will need a floor price and a ceiling price, i.e. match prices against competitors but go no lower than X or higher than Y.
- **Set pricing rule.** Match pricing, go lower by a certain amount or a certain percentage.

Repricing is an effective way to boost sales but will eat into your margins. Therefore, it should be used with caution. If incorrectly configured, pricing tools can sell your inventory at a massive loss or price you out of the market. Example repricing tools include Bqool[138].

---

138 http://affiliate.bqool.com/idevaffiliate.php?id=780

Creating Amazon listings

Matching against the Amazon catalogue

If a product you want to sell already exists on Amazon, you can add your offer to the product listing page. Each barcoded product should only have one entry in the catalogue.

To add an offer to a current product, a seller must specify the following information:

- Offer price.
- Quantity available.
- Condition (e.g. new or used).
- Shipping template (sets shipping prices and allowed destinations).

Product listings can be added in bulk by matching a list of barcodes against the Amazon catalogue. Some categories, brands and individual products are restricted, but most are available to all sellers.

Tip: To find products on Amazon, search for the barcode (also known as the EAN or European Article Number in the EU/UK and UPC or Universal Product Code in the USA). If no product exists, create a new listing.

Creating new listings

Only professional sellers can add products to Amazon's marketplace. In most categories, a product must have a unique identifier (e.g. a barcode like an EAN or a UPC). Along with the unique identifier, the seller must specify the following core information to create a product:

- Product name
- Manufacturer
- EAN (barcode)

- Description
- Category
- Photos

Other optional attributes are also available. In addition, Amazon's catalogue supports variations.

Amazon's listing system makes it easy to list new products. Sellers are free to create new products though, for some brands, new product listings (known as ASINs or Amazon Stock Identification Numbers) can only be created by the brand owner (as registered in Amazon Brand Registry). Products can either be added individually or via an upload file.

Whilst most categories require the product to be barcoded, Amazon's handmade programme lets artisans sell their handcrafted products directly to millions of Amazon customers all over the world.

Optimising product listings for search

Amazon product listings should contain high-quality content that gives consumers all the information they require to purchase. While the listing should be written primarily for consumers, the content must include appropriate keywords for relevant searches.

Keyword research

To appear for an Amazon search, a product listing must include the keywords in the query. Consequently, sellers need to include all relevant keywords when writing Amazon listings. When researching keywords for your Amazon listings, use the following sources:

- **Use your head.** Use your knowledge of the market and your experience as a consumer to brainstorm keyword ideas.
- **Website keywords.** If you have researched keywords for your website, you can use them in your Amazon listings.

- **Amazon Autocomplete.** If you enter a few letters in the Amazon search box, high volume search terms will automatically appear as suggestions.
- **Related items.** Look at products found under 'Customers who viewed this item also viewed.'
- **Competitor products.** The title and the product information of competitor products contain keywords that they think are important.
- **Keyword research tools.** Tools like Sellics Sonar[139] will give you a list of popular keywords by category and ASIN.

Writing compelling listings

There are several different elements to the Amazon listing. The most important are:

- **Title.** The product title is a maximum of 200 characters and you should aim for at least 80 characters. Include your top 5 keywords and capitalise each word.
- **Images.** Aim for at least five high-quality images (min 1000px on the longest side). The product should be on a white background for the main image and fill 85% of the picture.
- **Bullets.** Each listing can have up to five bullet points. These should highlight salient product features and include keywords.
- **Descriptions.** Minimum 150 words, giving more information about the products.
- **A+ Content.** An area of rich content available to brand owners.

Tip: When writing listings, remember that creating a readable product listing is essential for promoting the product and giving the customer the information they need to purchase. Write for the customer and not Amazon search.

---

139 https://sellics.com/sonar-amazon-keyword-tool

Amazon search

Amazon is one of the world's biggest search engines and rivals Google as the first port of call for consumers researching products.

As Amazon has grown, a new discipline of Amazon Search Optimisation has emerged, explicitly focusing on improving Amazon search performance.

What is Amazon search?

When a user searches on Amazon, Amazon will generate a list of the most relevant query results. The Amazon search algorithm is called A9 and has two equally important ranking factors:

- **Keyword optimisation.** A product can only be found by Amazon search if the product page contains the keyword(s) for which a customer is looking. Keyword optimisation ensures that a product can be found for all relevant keyword searches.
- **Listing performance.** How well a product ranks for these keywords depends on its performance metrics. The performance metrics are traffic and sales, click-through rate (CTR) and conversion rate (CR).

How Amazon ranks listings

How well a product ranks for these keywords depends on a listing's performance metrics. These include the listing's customer rating (product reviews and customer questions) and its sales performance.

- **Sales Rank.** More sales = higher rankings. Higher ranking = more sales!
- **Customer reviews.** The number of product reviews and the quality of these reviews are important ranking factors.
- **Price.** The price of your products strongly influences conversion rates and sales.

- **Click through and conversion rate.** Amazon looks at a listing's historical sales performance when ranking search results, including click-through and conversion rate.

Ranking Algorithm in a Nutshell

Step 1 — Filtration Process

Ranking Factor: Keywords

amazon | Enter Keyword

1-16 of 158.517.976 **Results**

amazon | White Sneakers

1-16 of 1.974.084 **Results in** "White Sneakers"

Step 2 — Sorting by Purchase Likelihood

Ranking Factor: Performance

Sales, CTR, CR — Images, Copy, Reviews, Ads, Traffic, Price, FBA/Prime, Inventory

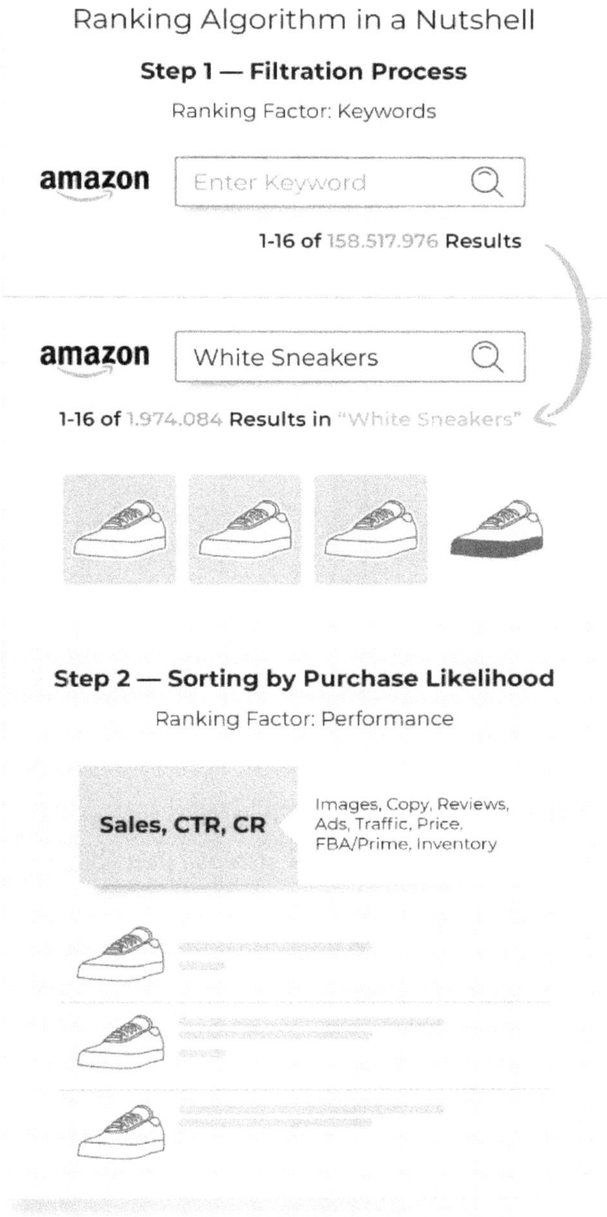

Fig. 52. How Amazon's search ranking algorithm works

Building sales history

Sales history influences the search performance of a listing. However, when a listing is new, it will not have any sales history. So, you can either wait for this to build naturally over time or use Amazon's Sponsored ads product to drive traffic to the listing and hopefully generate sales. We'll discuss Sponsored ads a bit later in this chapter.

A listing will more quickly build sales history by using sponsored ads, which will help it climb up the organic search rankings.

Improving Click-Through Rate and listing performance

A listing's click-through rate can improve by having high-quality content. This includes a compelling hero (main) image and product title. Listing optimisation is covered in the Creating Amazon Listing section above.

Gathering reviews

An essential component of increasing your listing performance is encouraging product reviews. You can increase your number of reviews in several ways.

- **Excellent customer service.** Both great and terrible customer service encourage reviews. You could also use parcel inserts to remind customers to leave reviews.
- **Amazon programs.** Amazon Vine is a paid-for program that enables brands to send new products to trusted Amazon reviewers to get early reviews.

- **Request review button.** Use Amazon's request review button on the order details page. This is guaranteed to ensure you stay within Amazon's T&Cs.
- **Send a review request.** This can be managed using tools such as Bqool, which automates the sending of review requests through the Amazon messaging system.

Amazon for brands

Brand registry

Amazon actively encourages brands to sell directly to Amazon customers and has launched various tools to enable rights owners to protect and promote their brand on Amazon. Brand Registry[140] enables brand trademark owners to register their brand with Amazon. Once the brand is registered, brand owners can do the following:

- Create a branded storefront.
- Run sponsored brand advertising campaigns.
- Add A+ content to listings.
- Remove counterfeit products.
- Amend listing details.
- Branded storefronts

A storefront displays the products available from a brand on Amazon. It has a vanity URL and is organised by category. In addition, configurable shop pages provide information and highlight products.

---

140 https://brandservices.amazon.com

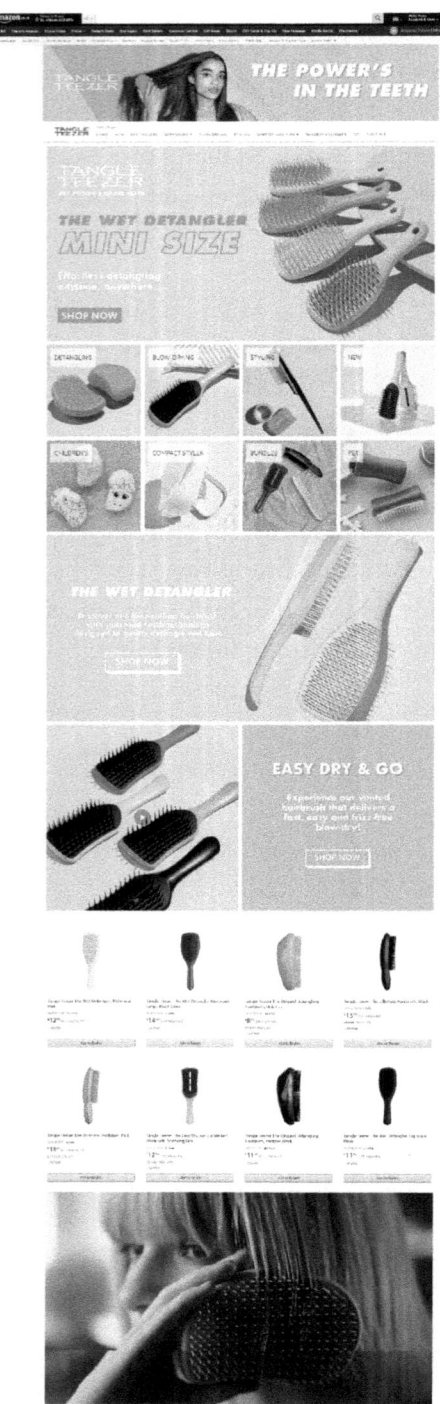

Fig. 53. Tangle Teaser's Amazon Storefront

A+ Content

A+ (or Enhanced Brand) Content is an area of rich media content added, by brand owners, to the product listing page. According to Amazon, adding A+ content can boost conversion rates by 5-10%

Fig. 54. A+ content for Tangle Teezer listing

Fulfilment method

Fulfilment is a significant factor on Amazon as it is a crucial factor in Buy Box ranking. Sellers can choose between Fulfilled by Amazon (FBA), Fulfilled by Merchant (FBM) and Seller Fulfilled Prime (SFP).

Fulfilled by Amazon (FBA)

FBA is Amazon's wildly popular fulfilment service. Items are stored in Amazon warehouses and shipped by Amazon to fulfil merchant orders. Amazon charges for storage and delivery[141], but these rates compare well with other fulfilment providers. FBA has four main advantages:

- **Easy.** Ship the products to Amazon and they do everything else. You do not need a warehouse or customer service staff.
- **Buy Box.** FBA orders get preference over FBM orders.
- **Prime eligible.** FBA orders are eligible for Amazon Prime.
- **No contracts.** FBA is pay-as-you-go – you only pay for what you use.

FBA is a great programme and makes much sense for retailers and brands selling to Amazon customers. However, it works best under the following circumstances:

- **Fast-moving product lines.** You do not want to be paying storage for products that are not selling.
- **Small catalogues.** Managing many items in small quantities in FBA is a headache.
- **Sturdy products.** Breakable products will not survive the process.

---

141 https://sell.amazon.co.uk/pricing?ref_=sduk_soa_priov_n#fulfillment-fees

FBA fees

There are four types of FBA fees:

- **Carrier fees.** Charged if you use one of Amazon's carrier partners to collect and deliver inventory to an Amazon fulfilment centre.
- **Storage fees.** These are charged based on the volume of inventory stored every month.
- **Fulfilment fees.** Each order incurs a fulfilment fee based on the size of the product.
- **Optional fees.** Amazon offers a range of product processing services that incur additional charges, e.g. re-barcoding, product furbishing.

Pan–EU FBA

The Pan-European FBA programme enables delivery of Prime eligible orders across the EU from a single inventory pool. Inventory is delivered to a single EU warehouse and fulfilment is charged at the local rate. To be enrolled in Pan EU FBA, a product must have a live listing on the 'EU4' (Amazon Germany, Italy, Spain and France).

For example, suppose you have a listing for a product live on the EU4 and deliver the inventory into Germany. In that case, the inventory level will be the same on each site (pooled inventory). When an order is placed, the fulfilment fee charged will be at the local rate of the site.

Tip: Pan-EU FBA is a great way to enable your inventory to be prime eligible across the whole of the EU.

Worldwide Fulfilled by Amazon (FBA)

The FBA programme is available in most countries where Amazon has operations and is available for international sellers. So, for example, a UK seller can use FBA in the US. However, they will need to manage the importing process including freight and customs clearance.

Tip: The ease of setting up with Amazon has heralded the launch of many 'FBA Brands' who only sell their products through Amazon FBA and no other channels. These products are produced in China and shipped directly to Amazon fulfilment houses. From there, Amazon does all the fulfilment and customer service.

Fulfilled by Merchant (FBM) and Seller Fulfilled Prime (SFP)

Fulfilled by Merchant is where the order is shipped directly from the seller to the customer. This gives the seller complete control, but FBM orders will be ranked lower than FBA offers, all things being equal.

A hybrid option is Seller Fulfilled Prime. SFP enables you to ship Prime eligible orders from your warehouse. This option has the advantages of FBA (Prime eligibility) without managing stock in two warehouses.

Shipping order via SFP has the potential to boost sales but has the following disadvantages:

- **Lack of control.** Amazon gives itself full right to refund Prime customers' orders for any reason. If you think that a refund is not justified, you need to put in a Safe-T claim to claw back the funds.
- **More returns.** Returns are authorised automatically for Prime members.

Amazon Sponsored Products

Amazon's Sponsored Product programme drives traffic to listings based on specified keywords. Sponsored Products ads are charged on a Pay Per Click (PPC) basis.

As mentioned above, Amazon search performance is primarily based on the listing's sale history. As new products do not have any history, buying traffic will often be necessary to build sales. You can scale back Sponsored Products Ads once the listing's natural sales performance picks up.

Amazon Sponsored Products works similarly to other PPC programs such as Google Ads, i.e.:

- An account is organised into campaigns and ad groups.
- Advertisers specify specific keywords to drive traffic to listings.
- Negative ad targets can also be added, e.g. keywords for which you do not want to appear.
- Bids are set at the Ad group or keyword level.

For example, a seller of iPhone cases might bid £0.5 to appear for the keyword 'iPhone 5S case'. However, they might only sell iPhone 5 cases, so use 'iPhone 6' and 'iPhone 7' as negative keywords.

There are several options within sponsored products:

- **Sponsored products.** Promote products to consumers who actively search with related keywords or view similar items on Amazon.
- **Sponsored brands.** Rich, engaging adverts that highlight your brand.
- **Sponsored display.** Rich display adverts promoting your brand or products.

Amazon for business

Amazon's 'Amazon for Business' program enables businesses to buy from Amazon and get the following benefits:

- VAT invoicing.
- Quantity discounts for bulk purchases (as specified by sellers).
- Request quote for bulk purchases from sellers.

To enroll in Amazon Business, a seller must be a VAT-registered business. They can then set quantity discounts based on the following criteria:

- Percentage discount based on order quality.
- Fixed price based on quantity.

Amazon says that selling to businesses through its platform can boost sales by 30%.

Sell globally

Most of Amazon's international sites are open to international (i.e. non-domestic) sellers. Each Amazon site works the same way. If you are familiar with one Amazon site, selling on international sites is straightforward.

As Amazon is a catalogue system, you may find that much of your inventory will already exist on international sites. This means that you will not need to translate your products and can get selling straight away. In addition, products should have the same ASIN in each country, so it is easy to identify the products you want to create.

The Pan European FBA programme allows you to deliver your inventory to one EU country but have Prime-eligible offers throughout the EU.

Summary

Love it or loathe it, Amazon is here to stay and offers an unparalleled platform for brands and retailers to reach more customers in the UK and internationally. Amazon has a presence in 20 countries and, as each site is similar, it is an easy way to expand your business overseas. Amazon is a catalogue-based site, meaning one listing for each product. Multiple sellers add their offer to each listing and these offers then compete to be the Featured Offer (a.k.a. winning the Buy Box). You will probably find that many products you sell are already available for sale on Amazon and adding your offer to an existing product is a great way to start making sales.

As the rise of 'FBA Brands' has shown, Amazon provides brands with an all-in-one launching pad for new brands. Brands can register their trademark for free and build a storefront to promote their brand on Amazon. However, with millions of products for sale, getting noticed is difficult. Fortunately, buying advertising through the Amazon Sponsored Product program is a quick (but expensive) way to build a sales history and collect reviews.

On the other hand, selling on Amazon is expensive and is an undignified experience. Amazon is very controlling and imposes strict and inflexible requirements on its sellers. Amazon is forever raising the standards it requires from its sellers, squeezing profits and making dealing with the customer more time-consuming.

10:

eBAY

eBay was my first eCommerce love and was the main reason I got into eCommerce. Its community of sellers and its feedback system are a throwback to the heady, early days of the Internet when individuals, rather than massive corporations, were in control. It is no longer a leader in eCommerce, but it is still a significant force with around 10% of the market. It is also a much more pleasant, less-mechanical place to do business than Amazon. eBay needs you. Amazon makes it quite clear that it does not.

While initially aimed at consumers, eBay's immense popularity quickly made it an excellent place for businesses to sell their products. The marketplace is particularly attractive to small businesses as it provides a one-stop shop for selling online. There is no need to set up a website or purchase additional advertising. Large companies such as Superdry, Currys, and Dyson sell on eBay alongside smaller sellers. This is due to its potential to sell distressed stock and promote products to an international audience.

Why businesses should sell on eBay

Opinion in the business community is divided about selling on eBay. Some businesses use eBay as a significant sales channel and become immersed in the community, proudly nurturing 100% feedback. Other companies feel that eBay is the equivalent of an online jumble sale and should be avoided at all costs.

Whilst eBay is no longer the leading eCommerce force, it is still a significant eCommerce player with 185 million users worldwide (Source: eBay[142]). Gross merchandising volume is a massive $100 billion/year (Source: eBay[143]). These figures are second only to Amazon, making eBay an opportunity every online seller should consider.

Benefits include:

One-stop-shop for selling online

eBay provides retailers with an easy solution for selling their products online. Many businesses find this a convenient solution as they do not need to go through the trouble of setting up a website and generating traffic.

International reach

As of 2019, eBay had a presence in 18 different countries. Consequently, selling on eBay opens a business to a massive international audience with the potential for increasing sales and acquiring customers.

Sell distressed stock

As well as selling new stock, eBay is a suitable place to sell distressed inventory such as returns or out-of-season products. Selling items in an online auction provides a greater return than traditional liquidation methods.

Promoted listings

eBay's Promoted Listing programme enables you to drive additional traffic to listings and only pay if a sale is made. When creating

---

142 https://investors.ebayinc.com/fast-facts/default.aspx
143 Ibid.

campaigns, you indicate how much additional commission you are happy to spend.

Drawbacks of selling on eBay

Fraud and fakes

Due to its position as an online bazaar, eBay has more than its fair share of 'bad actors.' Unfortunately, its openness and ease of use make it a magnet for fraudsters of all types. Problems on the eBay platform include:

- **Stolen accounts.** Fraudsters will steal the log-in details of genuine sellers and use their good reputation to sell non-existent products and disappear with the funds.
- **Stolen items.** eBay is sometimes used as a channel for disposing of stolen goods.
- **Items not as described.** There are 1.5 billion listings on eBay at any one time and a proportion will not be what they purport to be. Buyer beware.

The presence of fraud on eBay makes it doubly important for you to stand out from the crowd as a reputable business. Build your reputation by maintaining a healthy feedback score and presenting an image of a professional company with attractive listings, clear terms and conditions and contact details. On eBay, as in life in general, it is essential to remain vigilant, use common sense and suspect unusual behaviour.

Low prices

eBay is a place where buyers go to find bargains. Subsequently, there is fierce competition in the marketplace and prices there tend to be lower than on the high street and on the broader Internet. Many sellers on eBay are sole traders with low fixed costs and no requirement to charge VAT on their sales.

Time-consuming

It is time-consuming to sell on eBay and marketplaces in general. Marketplace customers are demanding and the presence of a feedback system requires their queries and grievances to be quickly addressed. eBay's listing system is also clunky when used with third-party listing tools.

Fees

Unfortunately, eBay is a business, and listing is not free. The eBay fees for each listing depend on the sale price, the type of listing used and the listings' success.

There are three types of eBay fees:

- **Insertion fee.** This fee is payable for listing an item on eBay, whether that item sells or not. Each seller is entitled to a certain number of free listings every month, depending on their subscription level (see eBay Shops below).
- **Listing upgrades.** eBay offers you several options for increasing the exposure given to items in the eBay search results. These include bolding the item's title in the search results or adding additional photos. Each of these upgrades incurs an additional fee per listing.
- **Final value fee.** If an item sells, eBay charges you a percentage of the item's final sale price.

Overall, eBay fees work out at about 10-15 % of the sale price (including shipping). This compares favourably with other online marketing channels.

eBay Shops

An eBay shop is a business' foothold on eBay and offers multiple options for promoting a company's products and brand.

Benefits include:

- **Storefront.** A shopping destination on eBay displays your inventory under one URL, e.g. stores.ebay.co.uk/hellobabydirect.
- **Branding.** The storefront has a logo and a customisable banner to promote a company's brand.
- **Listing discounts.** There are multiple shop subscription levels, each getting a quota of free listings.
- **International listings.** Upper shop levels get an allocation of free international listings.
- **Other freebies.** Other benefits include packaging vouchers.

eBay listing types

Auction Style

eBay became successful on the strength of its online auction business. eBay auctions work like traditional 'English' offline auctions where bidders compete to win an item. The highest bidder at the end of the auction is the winner.

Whereas offline English auctions do not end until the highest bid is placed, eBay auctions have a defined ending time, with the winner being the highest bidder when the clock stops. eBay auction listings can have a duration of 1, 3, 5, 7 or 10 days.

Auction listings can have the following additional options:

- **Buy it now.** The auction has a Buy It Now price (BIN), which disappears after the first bid.
- **Best offer.** Let buyers make offers. Allowing offers increases the chance of selling by 3-7% (Source: eBay).

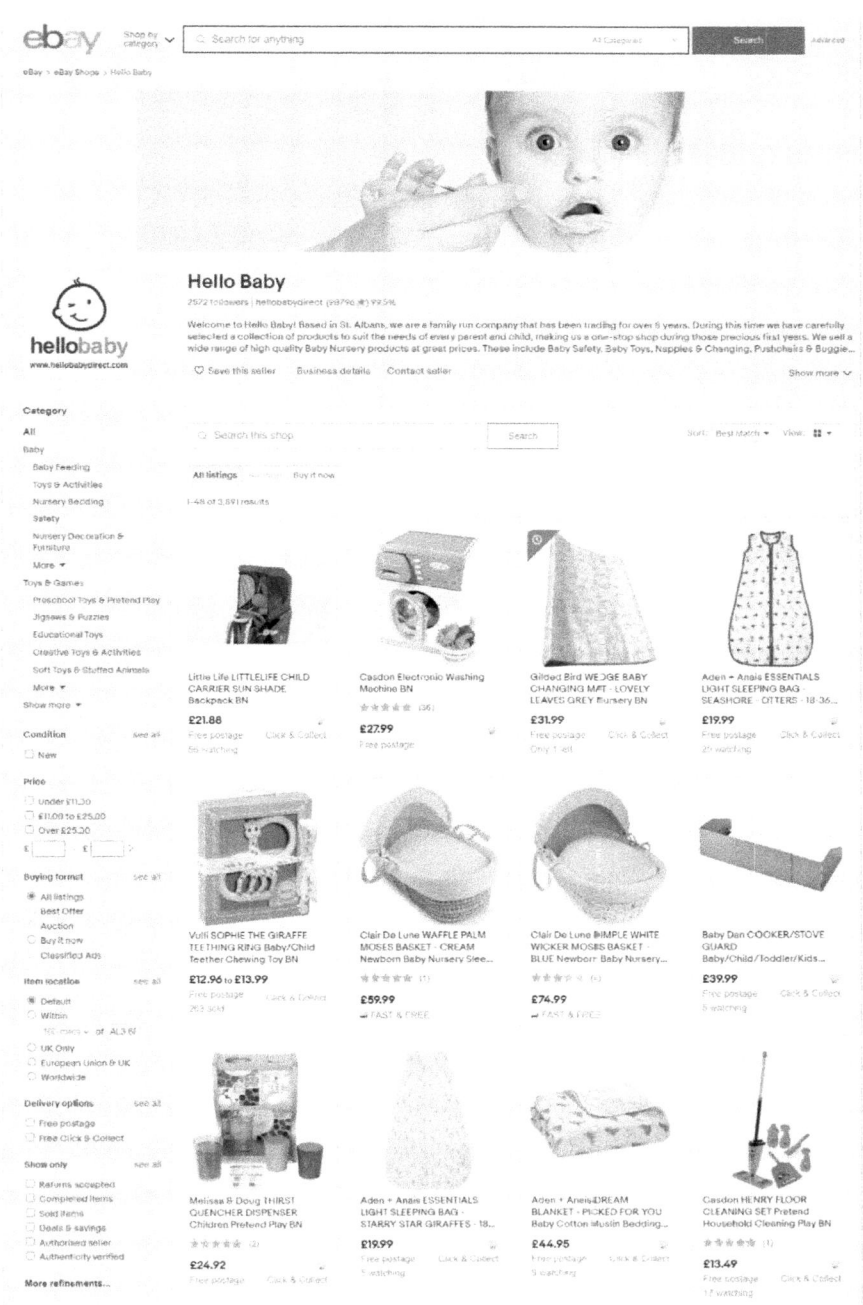

Fig. 55. Hello Baby's eBay Storefront.

Auction listings are best for selling second-hand, collectable or distressed stock where a quick sale is required.

Fixed price listings

Fixed Price listings allow buyers can purchase an item immediately at an advertised price. They are great for businesses selling new products and for individual sellers.

Fixed Price items have a duration of 30 days and you can specify the listing is 'Good 'til Cancelled', meaning that the listing renews automatically every 30 days.

Creating a listing

To list on eBay, you must complete several attributes that define the nature of the item for sale and the offer's details. These include:

- **Item category.** e.g. Baby > Baby Safety > Stair gates
- **Listing format.** e.g. Fixed price listing
- **Item title.** e.g. Clippasafe Auto Close Stair Gate Baby Safety BNIB
- **Item description.**
- **Postage options.** e.g. Royal Mail 1st Class

Item category

Each item must be in one of eBay's 13,000 categories, ranging from antiques to video games. There are 31 top-level categories, each of which has multiple sub-categories. If an item does not fit neatly into one category, it can be listed in two categories, although this doubles the listing fee.

Many buyers look for items by browsing a category, so choosing the right category helps attract potential buyers. The category also determines the item specifics available for a product. Item specifics are product attributes. They are used to filter searches which allow users to narrow down the results (see below).

Choosing a listing format

As mentioned above, eBay offers two main listing formats, i.e. fixed price and auction. Auctions are best for unique items such as antiques, whereas fixed price works best for selling new items.

Item title

The most critical part of an eBay listing is the title. Every eBay item has a title which is a maximum of 80 characters. This title is queried when users are searching for products and it also forms the name for the item in the eBay search results and the item profile page.

For items to get found, they must appear in searches relevant to your products. Despite eBay's introduction of the best-match search algorithm, finding items on eBay is still primarily driven by a keyword search of the title and description. It is therefore vitally important to write a compelling title for each product. By placing important keywords in an item's title, you can help potential buyers to find your items and improve sales.

Keywords can include:

- Manufacturer
- Brand
- Model number
- Features

Here is an example of good and bad eBay title for an iPhone X:

Good title: Apple iPhone X Space Grey 32GB Unlocked Original Box A1901 + Silicone Case
Bad title: Apple iPhone X + Case

The first title uses space appropriately, utilising 74 out of the available 80 characters for the item title. The second title wastes valuable space and does not correctly describe the item. An item will appear in fewer relevant search results if the keywords in the search query are not in an item's title and description.

When looking for keywords to include the titles, consult the following sources:

- **eBay autocomplete.** The eBay search bar autocompletes searches with high-volume phrases.
- **External keyword tools.** Keyword tools such as Google Keyword planner can suggest keywords for eBay titles.
- **Top eBay listings by category.** eBay Terapeak research tool gives top listing by category.

Item specifics

For many categories, eBay has defined a list of item specifics. These attributes can be attached to a listing to help people search. For example, item specifics for a laptop listing might include the make, model number and hard drive size. To narrow their searches, buyers can use the item specifics when browsing categories.

Description

While a good title and correct use of item specifics help drive buyers to a listing, a good description and photos will encourage a bid or a sale.

An item's description is a free text field where you have total freedom to describe the item in your own words. A good description should include all the information a buyer needs when purchasing an item. Remember that it is also an advert for the item and so it should sell the item by giving compelling reasons for making a purchase.

A good description should include:

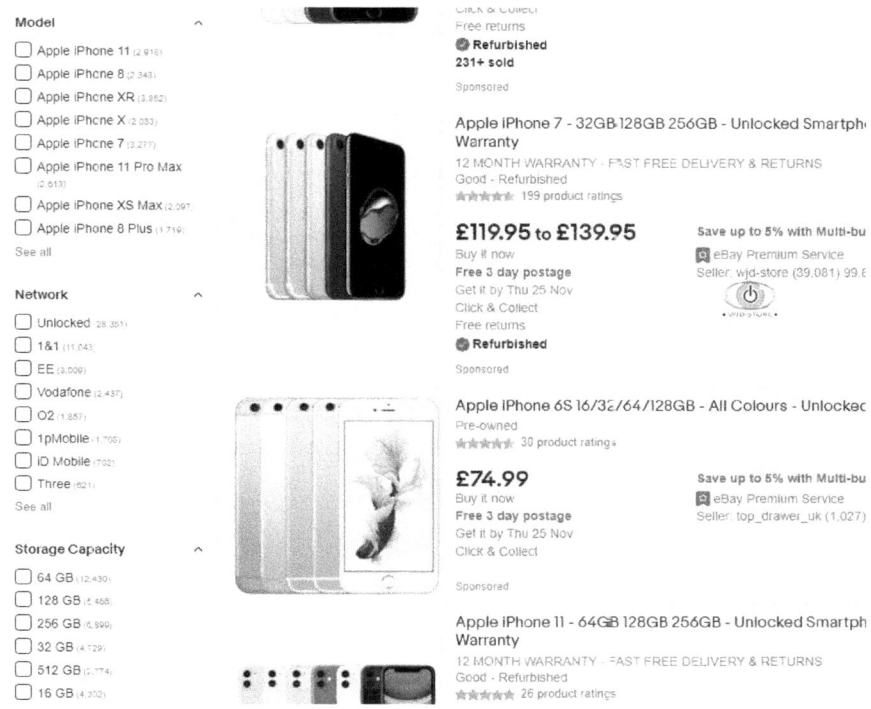

Fig.56. Search filters powered by item specifics on eBay search results

- **List of the item's features.** Do not assume that the buyer will be motivated enough to go and research the item for themselves.
- **Any faults.** It is easier to be upfront about an item at the start as it will reduce customer service issues and the number of questions received. Furthermore, misrepresenting an item is against eBay rules and will lead to negative feedback.
- **Other information.** It is worth adding information about payment and delivery options and any terms and conditions of sale.
- **Links.** Link to your eBay shop to encourage people to buy complementary items.

As the descriptions field of an eBay item supports HTML, it is possible to design an attractive listing that promotes your business.

Below is an example of a well-designed eBay listing:

Fig. 57. eBay listing using HTML

Images

As buyers of eBay items cannot physically see or touch an item, it is vital to provide them with quality pictures of your item. Images should be high resolution and the product should take up most of the picture. The main image should be on a white background. eBay allows buyers to submit up to 12 images for free.

eBay Best Match search

Buyers come to eBay items via several different routes:

- **Keyword search.** The most frequent method of finding products on eBay is via the eBay search. It searches the item's title (or, if specified, title and description) for keywords and produces a list of results ordered using eBay's Best Match algorithm (see below).
- **Category browsing.** Items can be found by browsing the items within a category. Potential buyers can filter by subcategories and item specifics to narrow the field.
- **Internal eBay Shop search.** Each eBay shop has its own search and category structure. This allows users to find the items they want within a shop.
- **Search engines.** eBay items appear in the natural search listings. eBay also purchases Google Ads to drive traffic to listings.

eBay orders its search results using its Best Match algorithm.

Best Match uses the following factors to determine the order of the search results:

- **Content Match.** Match between the search terms and the item's content.

- **Historical performance of the listing.** eBay gives higher placement to listings that have a sales history.
- **Seller Performance.** Measured by their detailed seller ratings and feedback.
- **Time to the end of the listing.** Applies only to auction listings.

Payment

eBay enabled sellers to offer a range of payment options for their listings until recently. The default option was PayPal, the popular online payment provider eBay once owned.

Since eBay sold PayPal in 2015, it has slowly developed its payment system called 'Managed Payments'. Managed payments allow customers to pay via various popular payment options, including PayPal, Apple Pay, Google Pay and Debit/Credit Card. The funds are deposited regularly into your bank account. Most eBay sellers are now using Managed Payments.

Feedback

Once the transaction is complete and the item dispatched, the counterparties can leave feedback for each other, commenting on how the trade went.

Feedback has three elements:

- **A comment,** e.g. Great eBayer, highly recommended!!!!
- **A mark.** Buyers can mark a transaction as a positive (+1), negative (-1) or neutral (0) experience. Sellers can only leave positive (+1 feedback).

- **Detailed seller ratings.** An item's buyer can mark a transaction 1 out of 5 on several criteria, including postage costs, delivery time and description accuracy.

The feedback information for individual transactions is collated over time to provide three metrics to users:

- **Feedback score.** The sum of all the individual feedback marks awarded.
- **Feedback percentage.** The percentage of positive feedback.
- **Average detailed seller rating.** The average of the detailed seller rating marks.

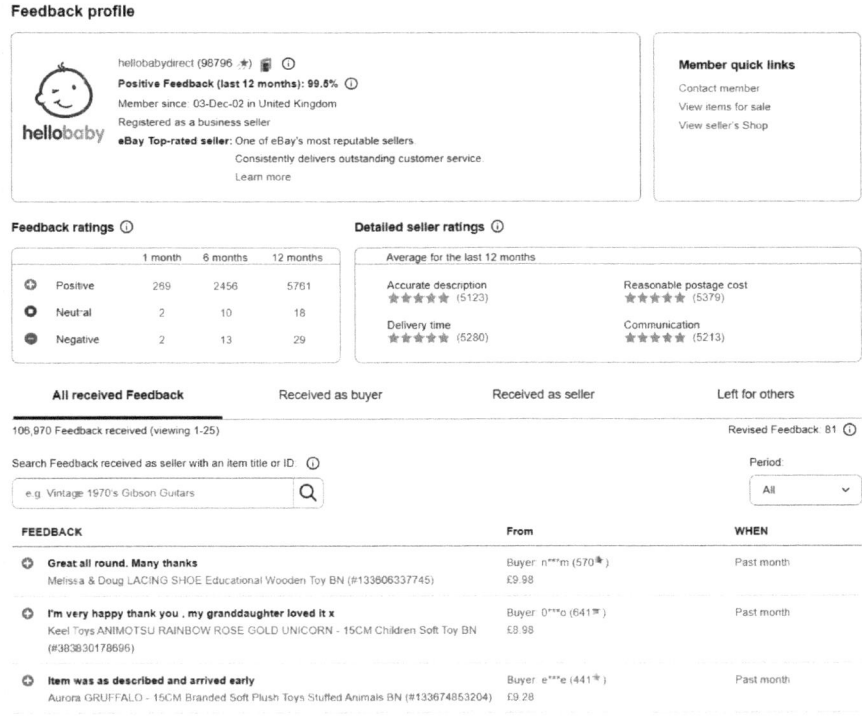

Fig. 58. eBay feedback profile

The feedback system is one of the reasons why eBay has become a global success. It reassures buyers that they are not dealing with a stranger but, instead, with a community member who has a trading history.

Feedback, however, is a blunt tool. Whilst it does indicate good customer service, all active traders above a certain size will have feedback of 98%+ which leaves little room for comparing relative performance.

As well as encouraging buyers to trade with you, a healthy feedback score will positively affect your eBay search performance. Conversely, if your account has a poor feedback score or detailed seller rating, its listings will be displayed lower in the search results.

Seller level

The eBay Seller Level is based on several performance metrics which measures the quality of service you give to buyers.

There are three levels:

- **Top Rated.** You are providing an excellent level of service and exceeding all standards.
- **Above Standard.** You are meeting the minimum standards.
- **Below Standard.** You are not meeting the minimum standards.

Your eBay Seller Standard is assessed every month and calculated for each trade region.

The metrics evaluated are:

- **Transaction defect rate.** The total percentage of transactions that had defects.
- **Cases closed without seller resolution.** If a buyer has a problem

with an order, they can start a case. If eBay must step in, this counts against you.

- **Late delivery rate.** An order is late if no tracking number was provided or the customer records the order, in the detailed seller ratings, as delivered late.

Top-Rated Seller is worth having as Top-Rated Sellers qualify for the 'Premium eBay Service' badge, giving a 10% discount on final value fees.

eBay Promoted Listings

eBay Promoted system is a simple yet effective advertising system for boosting your eBay sales. Unlike Amazon Sponsored Products or Google Ads, eBay Promoted Listings are not auction-based or keyword-targeted. Instead, you choose a level of additional commission to pay for the promoted listing. If the listing does not sell, there is no payment to make. Promoted Listings is an excellent programme for boosting your items in the search results and positively impacting sales.

How Promoted Listings work

To sponsor listings, specify the items you wish to promote and how much of the sale price you are willing to pay. eBay then boosts the listings from their usual search results to the four top spots in the eBay search results or placements lower down the page.

If a buyer clicks on a promoted listing and then buys it, you pay eBay the percentage you set when creating the campaign, in addition to the usual final value fee. If the item does not sell, there is nothing to pay. The typical range for successful listings is 5-10% of the sale price.

As you choose the additional commission you are willing to pay, the cost of eBay Promoted Listings is easy to control compared with PPC programmes such as Google Ads.

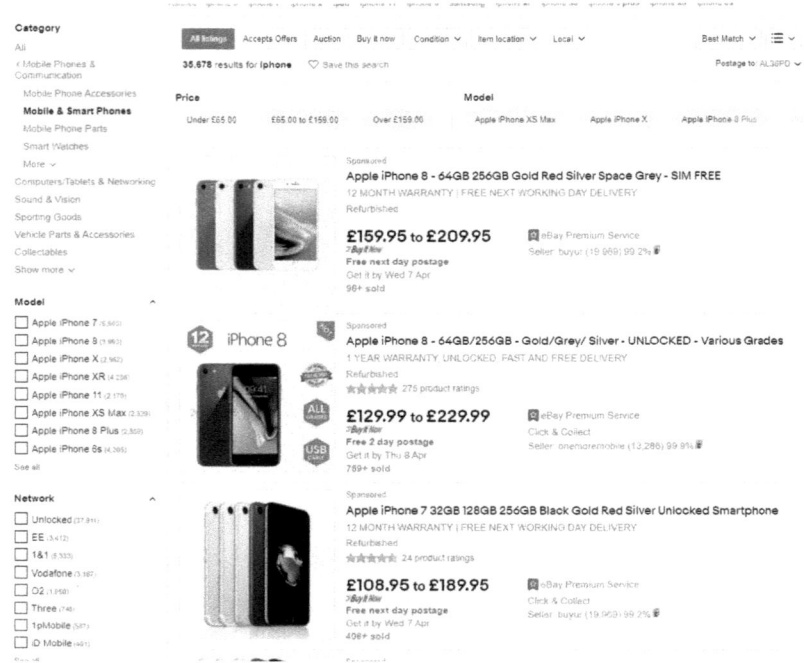

Fig. 59. Sponsored eBay listings

Promoted Listings best practice

eBay Promoted Listing can improve sales performance under several circumstances:

- **Bestsellers.** Items that have proven popular with customers will respond well to promotion if you are willing to sacrifice margin.
- **High conversion rate/low traffic items.** If you have listings that are converting well but have low sales, these could benefit from additional traffic from Promoted Listings.
- **New items.** eBay's Best Match search algorithm looks at the sales history of listings so promoting listings will help build listing history.
- **Liquidation.** Promoted listings can drive traffic to products that need to sell quickly.

International selling

eBay has customers worldwide and offering to ship purchases to international locations opens your products to a global market at no additional cost.

Standard international selling

The easiest way to sell internationally with eBay is to list products on your domestic eBay site but add international shipping options. The listings will then appear in the search results of regions for which shipping details are specified. On non-English sites, listings are translated automatically into the local language.

Advanced international selling

If you wish to localise your listings, you can publish them directly on international eBay sites. These listings will have higher visibility as they will appear in the search results on those local sites.

Creating your own listings allows you to translate item descriptions professionally into the local language and appeal to more buyers. The fees paid will be at the local country rate (not the domestic rate).

Global Shipping Programme

Shipping internationally can be a pain, especially now that the UK has left the EU and there is import VAT to consider. eBay's Global Shipping Programme aims to take the pain out of international shipping. Once you have joined the programme, customers worldwide can purchase your products and eBay will manage all the taxes and shipping fees. Then you need only ship the product to a UK fulfilment centre.

Market research

On the Seller Dashboard, eBay provides tools to help you improve listing performance and research opportunities on the eBay marketplace.

- **Product research.** Research top-selling products on eBay by keyword, category and listing.
- **Sourcing insights.** Popular eBay categories for you to research.
- **Listing improvements.** Listings where eBay recommends price reductions to improve competitiveness and the addition of item specifics to improve findability.
- **Restocking advice.** In-demand products from your inventory that are out of stock.

This data can improve eBay listing and help find popular products to sell on other channels.

Summary

eBay is a massive international marketplace with over 180 million active users worldwide. While eBay started as an online auction platform, most sales are now fixed-price items. Many brands avoid eBay as they view it as a low-value platform akin to an online garage sale. However, many of the world's biggest brands have outlets on eBay, including Dyson, BMW, Currys, Argos and Super Dry.

Selling on eBay is a straightforward process and is more accessible than setting up and advertising a website. eBay listings and shops allow you to promote your brand on eBay in a much less controlled way than Amazon. eBay's Promoted Listing advertising programme drives traffic to listings and builds sales history. As a listing's sale history builds, it will achieve better rankings in eBay's natural search, allowing you to reduce your advertising spend.

Resources

Translating eBay listings is hard to manage but listing locally will boost sales. Web Interpret (https://www.webinterpret.com) automates the process of translating and publishing listings for a sales commission (5%).

Optiseller (https://www.optiseller.com) is a tool for managing items specifics. It gives reports that detail missing specifics and this helps sellers optimise their listings.

11:

ALTERNATIVE MARKETPLACES

T he are many online marketplaces worldwide and, while still having a large customer base, these local champions often have lower competition than eBay and Amazon. Unfortunately, only a few are of genuine interest to Western sellers, either because they are too small or the setup and management is too complicated.

Onboarding on some marketplaces is much easier than in others. For example, marketplaces like Bol.com and Cdiscount in the EU are self-service, allowing you to launch your own account. Others, like Tmall in China, require the services of a local partner. Self-service marketplaces are much cheaper and easier to run.

Below is a (very) incomplete list of online marketplaces.

CDiscount

With 11 million unique visitors to the site every month, Cdiscount (www.cdiscount.com) is a significant marketplace in France. It offers products in over 40 distinct categories, operates a fulfilment service and has a network of 18,500 pickup points. CDiscount was launched in 1998 and is a household name among French shoppers. It is particularly well-known for electronics and tech products and is popular with tech-savvy shoppers looking for reasonable prices.

Pros: Major marketplace in France and the second most popular after Amazon. Catalogue-based system and so easy to list inventory against existing listings. Selling on CDiscount is simple as it integrates with most major eCommerce platforms.

Cons: Back end is hard to use.

Fruugo

Fruugo (www.fruugo.com) is a UK marketplace that connects buyers with products from all over the world. It launched in 23 countries in 2013. One of its primary selling points is that it uses a single feed to give you access to multiple countries worldwide.

Fruugo's marketplace automatically translates listings to 15 different languages, which removes the need to list items on numerous localised versions of a marketplace. Payment is on a commission basis with no monthly fees. Fruugo has around 1.5 million customers worldwide and is experiencing strong growth.

Pros: Easy to list products using a product feed. Great for international sales.

Cons: Back end can be challenging to use.

OnBuy.com

OnBuy (www.onbuy.com) is a fast-growing UK based marketplace. It offers much lower fees than other marketplaces (5 to 9%) and has a presence in 51 countries. Payments are managed via PayPal.

Pros: OnBuy's Catalogue-based system is easy to set up and integrates with most major eCommerce platforms. If you do not hit £500 in sales in a month, your subscription fee is refunded.

Cons: Small by comparison with the other marketplaces mentioned in this book.

Bol.com

Bol.com (www.bol.com) is an online marketplace and store which serves consumers in the Netherlands and Belgium. It operates in a comparable way to Amazon. Like Amazon, it sells directly to consumers and offers its platform as a marketplace where other online retailers can list products. Bol is based in the Netherlands and has a turnover of more than €1 billion.

Pros: The market leader in the Netherlands, one of Europe's largest economies. It is a catalogue based system, which makes product listing easy.

Cons: Picky about the sellers they accept. Rigorous performance metrics. The product creation process is complex.

Tmall and Taobao

Alibaba (www.alibaba.com), the Chinese eCommerce colossus, runs three enormous online marketplaces. Tmall is the domestic business-to-consumer marketplace, Tmall Global (www.tmall.com) is for international brands and Taobao (www.taobao.com) is a consumer-to-consumer eCommerce site. These marketplaces process a staggering number of transactions and boast a billion monthly users.

Selling on Tmall as a foreign company is complex and out of the reach of small to mid-sized retailers. To sell on the platform requires the following:

- Letters from suppliers stating the company has the right to sell that product in China.
- $25,000 deposit.

- Services of a Tmall Partner (TP). These cost about $5,000/ month.

Also, shipping into China is complicated and requires a specialist courier to ensure deliverability. Listing and customer service must also be localised into the Chinese language.

Pros: Enormous marketplace.

Cons: Challenging for small retailers to get started. Only interested in international brands.

Rakuten

Rakuten (www.rakuten.co.jp) is the biggest eCommerce site in Japan, with Amazon Japan a close second. Products are sold at a fixed price. However, unlike Amazon, it is a pure marketplace and does not sell its own products.

To sell on Rakuten requires a local partner's services and both customer service and product listing are in Japanese.

Pros: Biggest marketplace in one of the world's largest markets.

Cons: Requirements for a local partner makes it difficult and expensive to get started.

Allegro

Allegro (www.allego.pl) is the leading eCommerce platform in Poland and the fifth most visited European marketplace (Source: bvoh.de[144]).

144 https://bvoh.de/ranking-335-marketplaces-throughout-europe-online-means-diversity

The site has over 20 million customers and has been trading for over 20 years. Allegro has a significant market share in electronics (62%), home and garden (74%) and fashion (46%).

Brands of all sizes sell on Allegro. Some notable names include Superdry, Hollister, Abercrombie and designer labels e.g. Versace and small boutique brands.

Pros: Poland is a large marketplace where eBay and Amazon do not have much presence.

Cons: Many eCommerce platforms do not support Allegro. Much of the site is only available in Polish.

Mercado Libre

Mercado Libre (www.mercadolibre.com) is an online marketplace operating in 15 Latin American countries. It is the 7th most visited online retail site globally, with 175 million active users. Set up costs are low as it charges a percentage commission on items sold and does not charge a listing fee.

Mercado Libre operates a cross-border trade programme covering Brazil, Mexico, Argentina, Chile and Columbia. It offers automatic language translation which makes localisation easy.

Pros: South America is a vast marketplace where Amazon does not have a strong presence.

Cons: The postage system in South America is very unreliable so a specialist courier is required. Duty is also charged on most deliveries and is hard to calculate. If you utilize the cross-border trade programme, you will need to ensure that those products are compliant with local regulations. Unfortunately, most eCommerce platforms do not support it.

Lazada

Founded in 2012, Lazada (www.lazada.com) is Southeast Asia's leading eCommerce platform and has a presence in six countries – Indonesia, Malaysia, the Philippines, Singapore, Thailand and Vietnam. The company offers products in several categories, including consumer electronics, household goods, toys, fashion, sports equipment and groceries.

Cons: Postage systems in Asia are not as reliable as in the West. Lazada has got around this problem by developing a delivery network. All orders must be labelled using Lazada delivery labels and then bulk shipped to their Hong Kong processing hub. This makes shipping difficult as you need to factor in getting the item to Hong Kong and the charge that Lazada will make for their delivery services. The duty also needs to be factored in and varies by country and product class. Unfortunately, most eCommerce platforms do not support it.

Wish

Wish (www.wish.com) is a popular and growing online marketplace. Shoppers install the Wish app or visit the website to receive a scrolling shopping feed that is personalised to each shopper's browsing and buying behaviour. This customised feed makes the marketplace highly engaging and addictive for consumers while making it easy for sellers to get their goods in front of new and relevant audiences.

Pros: Fast-growing online marketplace which is mobile-focused. Wish has over 300 million users across over 120 different countries. It is particularly popular with younger people, with 60% of its customers Millennials or Generation Z.

Cons: Wish is a marketplace for bargain hunters looking to source cheap goods directly from Chinese manufacturers. Many products are of low quality. In addition, Wish imposes stringent performance rules and fines on its sellers. These can seem harsh to established retailers.

Another drawback is that shipping is slow. For example, 87% of Wish sellers deliver directly from China and consequently, customers frequently wait for between two and four weeks to receive their order.

Walmart

Walmart (marketplace.walmart.com) is the biggest retailer globally, but it had lagged way behind Amazon online until recently. However, it is investing heavily to catch up and has launched its marketplace for third-party sellers.

Walmart Marketplace has a longer onboarding process than platforms like Amazon and they do not accept all sellers. Merchants must either have a distribution hub in the US or use Walmart's fulfilment service (their version of FBA). It is not acceptable to use Amazon FBA to fulfil orders or send orders from overseas.

If you can fulfil the requirements for selling on Walmart, it represents a growing opportunity for online sellers. Walmart is the world's biggest retailer and has 140 million customers online and offline. It also offers a Prime-like subscription service and a fulfilment service.

Summary

eBay and Amazon are not the only marketplaces available and many regional champions are open to international sellers. These marketplaces can help reach customers outside the reach of eBay and Amazon in areas such as South America and Asia. However, onboarding onto these marketplaces can be tricky. Whenever you are looking to launch a new marketplace, ask the following questions

- **Is it worth it?** From experience, about 2 in 3 marketplaces do not generate sufficient sales to make them worthwhile.
- **Account setup.** Can you set up an account for this marketplace? Some platforms require stock to be stored domestically (e.g. Walmart) or sold by a local company (e.g. Bol.com).
- **Delivery.** Will you be able to deliver to this location reliably? For some regions (e.g. China, Russia, South America), a specialist courier will be necessary to ensure deliverability.
- **Funds.** How will you transfer funds to your domestic bank account if you make sales?
- **Integration.** Can the platform be integrated with your current systems? If not, stock and delivery issues are more likely and it will be more work to run.

One benefit of a marketplace that is more challenging to sell on is that there will be less competition. This will lead to higher sales and healthy margins. Sometimes it is good to be a big fish in a small pond.

Resources

If you want to remit funds received in foreign currencies, consider using a dedicated currency broker. They will offer a better rate, saving you money. Payoneer is a reliable international solution:

http://www.payoneer.com

The UK Department of International Trade (DIT) has a resource of international sales opportunities for online retailers:

https://www.great.gov.uk/selling-online-overseas

WRAPPING UP

Thanks for reading my book. I hope you enjoyed it! It has taken me 15 years to live it and two years to write it. Working for yourself is a rewarding journey and eCommerce is an excellent business! Online retail is nowhere near its full potential and we can look forward to many more years of solid growth.

To end, here is some general advice for people looking to launch or grow their business.

Get started

One of my regrets is that I did not start my entrepreneurial journey earlier. You learn valuable lessons, meet like-minded people and work out the best route for you and your company. It is never too soon to get going.

Have a DIY attitude

As an entrepreneur, you need to be ready to roll up your sleeves, do it yourself and give everything a go. I've managed my SEO, PPC and marketplaces as well boring stuff like Human Resources and accounts. This has saved me a fortune and given me valuable knowledge. Now that my business is too big for me to do everything, this comprehensive knowledge of my industry puts me in a better position to manage my team and external suppliers.

Maximise opportunities

If you offer a product or service, advertise it in as many places as possible to maximise the potential market. For example, at Hello Baby, we sell our products through more than 20 channels worldwide. The channels all generate additional sales which add to the bottom line.

Start small

The concept of the lean start-up[145] applies to most areas of business. Limit your exposure by testing the water. Before launching a website, buy small stock quantities, run test campaigns and sell on marketplaces. Always use off the shelf products to run your business (e.g. Shopify) as this will get your company up and running quickly and cheaply.

Keep costs low

As an entrepreneur, money may be tight. However, you probably do not need half the things on which you spend money. For example, I have often found that software that costs £1000/month has an alternative that costs less than £100. Always shop around!

Stay in touch!

Please feel free to get in touch if you have any questions about the topics covered in this book. You can reach me at trevor@vendlab.com. Please also join our Facebook group[146] to talk with like-minded people.

If you need in-depth help, I have a range of eCommerce courses available on Udemy[147], the eCommerce Odyssey Podcast[148] and VendLab eCommerce School[149] YouTube Channel. In addition, I run an eCommerce Consultancy called VendLab[150].

Good luck!

---

145 http://theleanstartup.com/principles
146 https://www.facebook.com/groups/vendlab
147 https://www.udemy.com/user/trevor-ginn-2/
148 https://vendlab.com/podcasts/
149 https://www.youtube.com/c/VendlabeCommerceSchool/
150 https://vendlab.com/

About the author

Trevor Ginn is an entrepreneur and eCommerce nut with 15 years of hands-on experience selling online. He is the founder of Hello Baby, a leading online retailer in the baby and nursery space which he built from scratch to a turnover of £5m/year.

Hello Baby has customers worldwide and trades successfully on Amazon, eBay, Google Shopping and other international channels.

Alongside his retail business, Trevor runs VendLab (www.vendlab.com), an eCommerce agency that specialises in multi-channel global eCommerce.

Trevor loves climbing, mountain biking, scouting, and reading when not thinking about eCommerce.

More from the author:

Udemy Courses: https://www.udemy.com/user/trevor-ginn-2/

Facebook group: https://www.facebook.com/groups/vendlab/

Consulting + Newsletter: https://www.vendlab.com

Ecommerce Odyssey Podcast: https://rss.com/podcasts/ecommerce-odyssey/

YouTube Channel: https://www.youtube.com/c/VendlabeCommerceSchool

Acknowledgements

Thanks to the following people for their help with writing this book:

My lovely family Christina, Lara & Scarlett

Tom Horner

Chris Cartwright

Douglas Williams

My parents: June and Mike Ginn

Dan Prescott at Couper Street Type Co.